I CAN
초등 영단어
Advanced
Level

단어 1000 + 문장 1000

by HWA KYUNG CHOI

KB097992

RINA
BOOKS

저자 **최화경**

영국에서 TESOL 과정을 수료

유럽 및 영어권 전문 영어가이드로 활동하고 있으며 번역가로도 활동하고 있다.

저서로는 [Block voca]가 있으며 번역 작품으로는 [영어와 함께 읽는 이솝우화]가 있다.

I can 초등 영단어
단어1000+문장1000

초판 1쇄 발행 | 2021년 12월 10일

저　자 | 최화경

펴낸이 | 이원호

펴낸곳 | 리나북스

등　록 | 제99-2021-000013호

주　소 | 경기도 남양주시 와부읍 덕소로97 101, 104-902

전　화 | 031)576-0959

이메일 | rinabooks@naver.com

구입문의 | rinabooks@naver.com

I S B N | 979-11-974084-5-8　63740

시작 글

단어는 영어 학습에서 기초를 이루는 핵심입니다.

단어를 많이 알수록 영어 실력은 높아집니다.

I can

초등 영단어

단어 1000 + 문장 1000은 단어의 정확한 의미나 쓰임을 알지 못해

문장을 이해하기 힘든 부분을 훈련시켜 줍니다.

I can

초등 영단어

단어 1000 + 문장 1000은 문제의 난이도를 높였습니다.

배움에 있어 난이도는 중요합니다.

문제를 풀면서 배우는 학습 효과는 단순 외우는 단어학습과는 다릅니다.

I can

초등 영단어

단어 1000 + 문장 1000은

예비 중학생을 위한 최고의 영어 준비서가 될 것입니다.

책의 구성

1일 20개, 50일 1,000개의 단어와 문장을 학습하도록 구성되어 있습니다.
5일 100개의 단어를 학습하면 Review Test 1,2를 통해 한주간의 학습을 완성합니다.

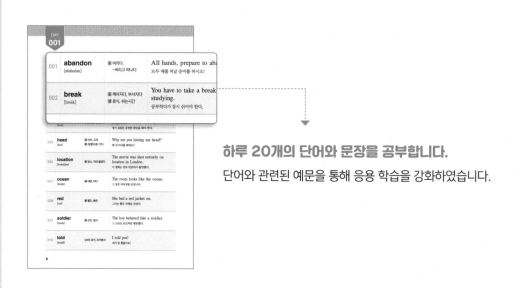

하루 20개의 단어와 문장을 공부합니다.

단어와 관련된 예문을 통해 응용 학습을 강화하였습니다.

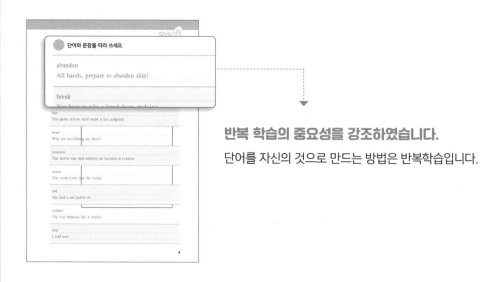

반복 학습의 중요성을 강조하였습니다.

단어를 자신의 것으로 만드는 방법은 반복학습입니다.

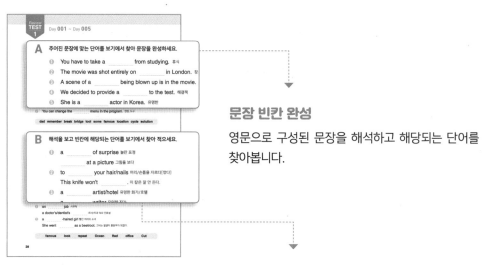

문장 빈칸 완성

영문으로 구성된 문장을 해석하고 해당되는 단어를 찾아봅니다.

표현 빈칸 완성

영문으로 구성된 다양한 표현을 해석, 공통으로 들어갈 단어를 찾아봅니다.

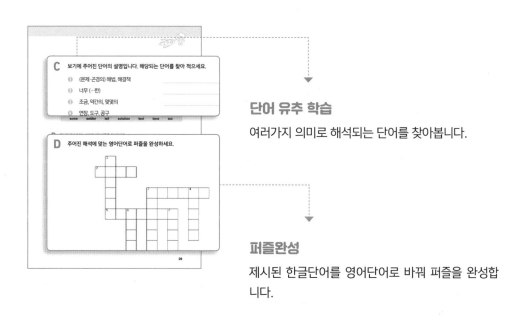

단어 유추 학습

여러가지 의미로 해석되는 단어를 찾아봅니다.

퍼즐완성

제시된 한글단어를 영어단어로 바꿔 퍼즐을 완성합니다.

목차

I CAN
초등 영단어
Advanced
Level

단어 1000 + 문장 1000

001	**abandon** [əbǽndən]	통 버리다, ~버리고 떠나다	All hands, prepare to abandon ship! 모두 배를 떠날 준비를 하시오!
002	**break** [breik]	통 깨어지다, 부서지다 명 휴식, 쉬는시간	You have to take a break from studying. 공부하다가 잠시 쉬어야 한다.
003	**crowd** [kraud]	명 사람들, 군중, 무리	The movie star drove the crowd. 영화배우는 군중들을 몰고 다녔다.
004	**fair** [fɛər]	형 공정한, 공평한	The game referee shall make a fair judgment. 경기 심판은 공정한 판단을 해야 한다.
005	**head** [hed]	명 머리, 고개 통 (방향으로) 가다	Why are you hitting my head? 왜 내 머리를 때려요?
006	**location** [loukéiʃən]	명 장소, 야외 촬영지	The movie was shot entirely on location in London. 이 영화는 전부 런던에서 촬영했다.
007	**ocean** [breik]	명 대양, 바다	The room looks like the ocean. 그 방은 바다처럼 보입니다.
008	**red** [red]	형 빨간, 붉은	She had a red jacket on. 그녀는 빨간 자켓을 입었다.
009	**soldier** [breik]	명 군인, 병사	The boy behaved like a soldier. 그 소년은 군인처럼 행동했다.
010	**told** [tould]	tell의 과거, 과거분사	I told you! 내가 말 했잖아요!

● 단어와 문장을 따라 쓰세요.

abandon

All hands, prepare to abandon ship!

break

You have to take a break from studying.

crowd

The movie star drove the crowd.

fair

The game referee shall make a fair judgment.

head

Why are you hitting my head?

location

The movie was shot entirely on location in London.

ocean

The room looks like the ocean.

red

She had a red jacket on.

soldier

The boy behaved like a soldier.

told

I told you!

011	**able** [éibl]	형 재능 있는, 능력 있는	He is able to write his name. 그는 자기 이름을 쓸 수 있다.
012	**bridge** [bridʒ]	명 다리	A scene of a bridge being blown up is in the movie. 다리가 폭파되는 장면이 영화에 나온다.
013	**cry** [krai]	동 울다, 외치다.	I made my younger brother cry. 나는 내 남동생을 울렸다.
014	**fall** [fɔl]	동 떨어지다, 빠지다, 내리다	The rain continued to fall all afternoon. 비가 오후 내내 내렸다.
015	**hear** [hiər]	동 듣다, 들리다.	I can't hear very well. 나는 귀가 잘 안들린다.
016	**log** [lɔ(:)g]	동 일지에 기록하다.	Make sure you log out and finish in the PC room. PC방에서는 꼭 로그 아웃하고 끝내야 한다.
017	**off** [ɔ:f]	부 멀리, 무엇이 제거됨	I need some time off. 나는 쉴 시간이 필요해.
018	**region** [rí:dʒən]	명 지역, 지방	This region has an odd custom. 그 지방에는 오래된 관습이 있다.
019	**solution** [səlú:ʃən]	명 해법, 해결	We decided to provide a solution to the test. 우리는 시험에 대한 해결책을 제공하기로 했다.
020	**tone** [toun]	명 어조, 말투	She spoke in a silky tone. 그녀는 부드러운 어조로 말을 했다.

able

He is able to write his name.

bridge

A scene of a bridge being blown up is in the movie.

cry

I made my younger brother cry.

fall

The rain continued to fall all afternoon.

hear

I can't hear very well.

log

Make sure you log out and finish in the PC room.

off

I need some time off.

region

This region has an odd custom.

solution

We decided to provide a solution to the test.

tone

She spoke in a silky tone.

021	**about** [əbáut]	분 거의 전 …에 대한	I heard a lot about you. 당신에 대해 많이 들었어요.
022	**bright** [brait] 브라이튼	형 선명한, 밝은, 눈부신	I like bright colors. 나는 밝은 색상을 좋아한다.
023	**cut** [kʌt]	동 베다, 자르다, 절개하다	I cut my nails too closely. 나는 손톱을 너무 짧게 깎았다.
024	**famous** [féiməs]	형 유명한	She is a famous actor in Korea. 그녀는 한국에서 유명한 배우이다.
025	**heard** [hə:rd]	동 hear의 과거·과거분사	I just heard the news. 나는 방금 소식을 들었습니다.
026	**lone** [loun]	형 혼자인, 단독의	a lone traveler. 혼자 여행하는 사람
027	**offer** [ɔ́:fər]	명 제의하다, 권하다.	I will offer him a fair amount. 나는 그에게 상당한 금액을 제안할 것이다.
028	**remember** [rimémbər]	동 기억하다, 기억나다	I remember seeing him somewhere. 그를 어디에선가 본 기억이 난다.
029	**solve** [salv]	동 해결하다, (문제를) 풀다.	We need to solve environmental problems. 우리는 환경문제를 해결해야 한다.
030	**too** [tu:]	분 그것도, 너무	He's going too fast. 그는 너무 빨리 가고 있다.

about

I heard a lot about you.

bright

I like bright colors.

cut

I cut my nails too closely.

famous

She is a famous actor in Korea.

heard

I just heard the news.

lone

a lone traveler.

offer

I will offer him a fair amount.

remember

I remember seeing him somewhere.

solve

We need to solve environmental problems.

too

He's going too fast.

031	**above** [əbΛv]	젠 ~보다 많은, ~을 넘는, ~보다 위에	The birds are flying above the ocean. 새들이 바다 위를 날고 있다.
032	**bring** [briŋ]	동 가져오다, 데려오다	I'll bring a book. 내가 책을 가지고 올께.
033	**cycle** [sáikl]	명 자전거, 오토바이 명 순환	We must break the vicious cycle quickly. 악순환을 빨리 끊어야 한다.
034	**far** [faːr]	부 멀리, ~ 떨어져	We didn't go far. 우리는 멀리 가지 않았다.
035	**heart** [haːrt]	명 심장, 가슴	She returned with a heavy heart. 그녀는 무거운 마음을 안고 돌아왔다.
036	**long** [lɔːŋ]	형 길이[거리]가~ 긴 부 오래, 오랫동안	She has long dark hair. 그녀는 검고 긴 머리를 갖고 있다.
037	**office** [ɔ́ːfis]	명 근무처, 사무실, 사옥	She works at the local post office. 그녀는 지역 우체국에서 일한다.
038	**repeat** [ripíːt]	동 반복하다	The more you repeat, the better. 반복할 수록 더 좋아진다.
039	**some** [səm]	한 약간의/조금 대 몇몇, 몇 개	Save some food for me. 내 음식을 조금 남겨줘.
040	**took** [tuk]	동 Take의 과거	He took her hand. 그는 그녀의 손을 잡았다.

above

The birds are flying above the ocean.

bring

I'll bring a book.

cycle

We must break the vicious cycle quickly.

far

We didn't go far.

heart

She returned with a heavy heart.

long

She has long dark hair.

office

She works at the local post office.

repeat

The more you repeat, the better.

some

Save some food for me.

took

He took her hand.

041	**academic** [ækədémik]	형 학업의, 학교의	He has an academic attitude. 그는 학구적인 태도를 가지고 있다.
042	**broke** [brouk]	형 부러지다.	His right arm broke. 그의 오른팔이 부러졌다.
043	**dad** [dæd]	명 아빠	I miss my dad a lot. 아빠가 많이 보고 싶다.
044	**farm** [fa:rm]	명 농장, 농원 동 농사를 짓다. 기르다.	There's an old farm over the hill. 언덕 넘어에 오래된 농장이 하나 있다.
045	**heat** [hi:t]	명 열, 열기 동 뜨겁게	He was overcome by the heat. 그는 더위에 지쳐있었다.
046	**look** [luk]	동 보다, 바라보다 동 찾다, 찾아보다	He does look tired. 그는 피곤해 보인다.
047	**often** [ɔ́:fən]	부 자주, 흔히, 보통	They often go fishing. 그들은 자주 낚시를 간다.
048	**reply** [riplái]	동 응하다, 대응하다, 대답하다	Please reply quickly. 빨리 답장해 주세요.
049	**son** [sʌn]	명 아들	He has a grown-up son. 그에게는 장성한 아들이 있다.
050	**tool** [tu:l]	명 연장, 도구, 공구	You can change the tool menu in the program. 프로그램에서 도구 메뉴를 변경할 수 있다.

academic
He has an academic attitude.

broke
His right arm broke.

dad
I miss my dad a lot.

farm
There's an old farm over the hill.

heat
He was overcome by the heat.

look
He does look tired.

often
They often go fishing.

reply
Please reply quickly.

son
He has a grown-up son.

tool
You can change the tool menu in the program.

051	**accident** [ǽksidənt]	똉 (자동차)사고	A rainy evening car accident occurred. 비오는 저녁 교통사고가 났다.
052	**brother** [brʌðər]	똉 형, 남동생	My brother is a man of wisdom. 형은 지혜로운 사람이다.
053	**damage** [dǽmidʒ]	똉 손상, 피해	The fire is a lot of damage. 화재로 피해가 심하다.
054	**fast** [fæst]	묌 빨리, 빠르게 똉 빠른	Do you always eat so fast? 항상 그렇게 빨리 드세요?
055	**heavy** [hévi]	똉 무거운, 육중한	He put the heavy book down. 그는 무거운 책을 내려 놓았다.
056	**lost** [lɔːst]	똉 길을 잃은, 잃어버린	I was lost on my trip to London. 런던 여행중에 나는 길을 잃었다.
057	**oh** [ou]	깝 오, 어	Oh, that's great news! 오, 굉장한 소식이네!
058	**represent** [rèprizént]	똥 대신하다, 대변하다.	What does this picture represent? 이 그림은 무엇을 의미하고 있습니까?
059	**soon** [suːn]	묌 빨리, 곧, 머지않아, 이내	I'll come and see you soon. 곧 널 보러 갈게.
060	**top** [tap]	똉 맨 위, 정상 똉 최고의	He got the top job. 그는 최고의 직장에 다녔다.

accident
A rainy evening car accident occurred.

brother
My brother is a man of wisdom.

damage
The fire is a lot of damage.

fast
Do you always eat so fast?

heavy
He put the heavy book down.

lost
I was lost on my trip to London.

oh
Oh, that's great news!

represent
What does this picture represent?

soon
I'll come and see you soon.

top
He got the top job.

061	**act** [ækt]	뗑 (특정한) 행동 통 행동을 취하다	You ought to act your age! 너의 나이에 맞게 행동해야한다!
062	**brought** [brɔːt]	통 bring의 과거, 과거분사	I brought some flowers for you. 너에게 주려고 꽃을 가지고 왔다.
063	**dance** [dæns]	뗑 춤, 무용	She's learning to dance. 그녀는 춤을 배우고 있다.
064	**fat** [fæt]	혱 뚱뚱한, 살찐, 비만인 뗑 지방	There is too much fat in processed foods. 가공 식품에는 지방이 너무 많다.
065	**help** [help]	통 돕다, 거들다 뗑 도움	Can I help you? 제가 도와 드릴까요?
066	**lot** [lat]	때 많음, 다량, 다수	She feels the cold a lot. 그녀는 추위를 많이 탄다.
067	**oil** [ɔil]	뗑 석유, 기름	I have to put oil in my car. 나는 자동차에 기름을 넣어야 한다.
068	**rest** [rest]	뗑 다른 사람들, 나머지 뗑 휴식, 휴양	I'm going to rest at home. 나는 휴식하기 위해 집으로 갔다.
069	**sound** [saund]	뗑 소리, 음	Could you turn the sound up? 소리를 좀 키워줄래?
070	**total** [tóutl]	혱 총, 전체의	In total, 200 parts are needed. 합쳐서 200개의 부품이 필요하다.

act

You ought to act your age!

brought

I brought some flowers for you.

dance

She's learning to dance.

fat

There is too much fat in processed foods.

help

Can I help you?

lot

She feels the cold a lot.

oil

I have to put oil in my car.

rest

I'm going to rest at home.

sound

Could you turn the sound up?

total

In total, 200 parts are needed.

071	**active** [ǽktiv]	형 활동적인, 적극적인	There are many active animals at night. 밤에 활동적인 동물들이 많다.
072	**brown** [braun]	형 갈색, 갈색인	I look good in brown clothes. 나는 갈색 옷이 잘 어울린다.
073	**danger** [déindʒər]	명 위험, 위험한 사람	They will be in danger. 그들은 위험에 빠질 것이다.
074	**father** [fáːðər]	명 아버지, 아버지 같은 사람 동 아버지가 되다	He's a very involved father. 그는 매우 착실한 아버지다.
075	**her** [hə]	대 그녀	Her daughter is very dear to her. 그녀의 딸은 그녀에게 매우 소중하다.
076	**loud** [laud]	형 큰, 시끄러운	She spoke in a loud voice. 그녀가 큰 소리로 말했다.
077	**old** [ould]	형 늙은, 나이 많은	There is an old teddy bear. 오래된 테디베어가 있다.
078	**result** [rizʌlt]	명 결과, 결실	He was delighted at the result. 그는 그 결과에 기뻐했다.
079	**south** [sauθ]	명 남쪽, 남부	They live on the south coast. 그들은 남부 해안지역에 산다.
080	**touch** [tʌtʃ]	동 만지다, 접촉하다.	Don't touch it, it's very dangerous. 만지지 마세요, 매우 위험합니다.

active

There are many active animals at night.

brown

I look good in brown clothes.

danger

They will be in danger.

father

He's a very involved father.

her

Her daughter is very dear to her.

loud

She spoke in a loud voice.

old

There is an old teddy bear.

result

He was delighted at the result.

south

They live on the south coast.

touch

Don't touch it, it's very dangerous.

081	**actor** [ǽktər]	명 배우	From my childhood I wanted to be an actor. 어린시절부터 나는 배우가 되고 싶었습니다.
082	**build** [bild]	동 만들어 내다, 건물을 짓다. 명 (사람의) 체구	Most children build a sandcastle. 대부분의 아이들이 모래성을 만든다.
083	**dark** [da:rk]	형 어두운, 캄캄한	He wears a dark suit. 그는 어두운 옷을 입고 있었다.
084	**favor** [féivər]	명 호의, 친절	I wish to ask a favor of you. 한 가지 부탁이 있습니다.
085	**here** [hiər]	부 여기에, 지금 감 여기요	What's going on here? 이곳에 무슨일이 있는거죠?
086	**love** [lʌv]	명 사랑 동 사랑하다	I love traveling by train. 나는 기차를 타고 여행하는 것을 좋아한다.
087	**on** [ɑ:n]	전 …(위)에 부 (쉬지 않고) 계속하여	she put the book on the table. 그녀는 책을 테이블 위에 놓았다.
088	**rich** [ritʃ]	형 부유한, 돈 많은, 부자인	Not all rich people are happy. 부자라고 다 행복하지 않다.
089	**space** [speis]	명 공간, 우주 동 간격을 두다	I needed space to be myself. 나 혼자 있을 공간이 필요하다.
090	**toward** [tɔ:rd]	전 ~ 쪽으로, ~을 향하여	She headed toward her desk. 그녀는 자신의 자리로 향했다.

단어와 문장을 따라 쓰세요.

actor

From my childhood I wanted to be an actor.

build

Most children build a sandcastle.

dark

He wears a dark suit.

favor

I wish to ask a favor of you.

here

What's going on here?

love

I love traveling by train.

on

she put the book on the table.

rich

Not all rich people are happy.

space

I needed space to be myself.

toward

She headed toward her desk.

091	**add** [æd]	통 첨가, 추가하다, 덧붙이다 통 수,양을 합하다	Add two teaspoons of salt. 소금 두 티숟가락을 넣어주세요.
092	**burn** [bəːrn]	통 타오르다, 불에타다	The water is hot, be careful not to burn yourself. 물이 뜨거워, 화상을 입지 않게 조심해.
093	**day** [dei]	명 하루, 낮, 날	I bathe every day. 나는 매일 목욕을 한다.
094	**fear** [fɪr]	명 공포, 두려움, 무서움	The child cried in fear. 아이는 무서워서 울었다.
095	**hide** [haid]	통 숨다, 감추다	Don't hide your feelings. 너의 감정을 숨기지 마라.
096	**low** [lou]	형 낮은, 아랫부분의 부 낮게, 아래로	The sun was low in the sky. 해가 하늘아래 낮게 떠 있다.
097	**once** [wʌns]	부 한 번, 언젠가	She comes to see us once a week. 그녀는 일주일에 한 번 우리를 보러온다.
098	**ride** [raid]	통 타다, 승마하다	The man is going to ride his bike. 남자가 오토바이를 타려고 한다.
099	**speak** [spiːk]	통 말하다, 이야기하다.	Do you speak English? 영어 할 수 있나요?
100	**town** [taun]	명 소도시, 읍	David lives in a small town. 데이빗은 작은 도시에 산다.

add

Add two teaspoons of salt.

burn

The water is hot, be careful not to burn yourself.

day

I bathe every day.

fear

The child cried in fear.

hide

Don't hide your feelings.

low

The sun was low in the sky.

once

She comes to see us once a week.

ride

The man is going to ride his bike.

speak

Do you speak English?

town

David lives in a small town.

A 주어진 문장에 맞는 단어를 보기에서 찾아 문장을 완성하세요.

① You have to take a _____ from studying. 휴식

② The movie was shot entirely on _____ in London. 장소에서~

③ A scene of a _____ being blown up is in the movie. 다리

④ We decided to provide a _____ to the test. 해결책

⑤ She is a _____ actor in Korea. 유명한

⑥ I _____ seeing him somewhere. 기억하다

⑦ We must break the vicious _____ quickly. 순환

⑧ Save _____ food for me. 조금, 일부

⑨ I miss my _____ a lot. 아빠

⑩ You can change the _____ menu in the program. 연장, 도구

> **dad remember break bridge tool some famous location cycle solution**

B 해석을 보고 빈칸에 해당되는 단어를 보기에서 찾아 적으세요.

① a _____ of surprise 놀란 표정
_____ at a picture 그림을 보다

② to _____ your hair/nails 머리/손톱을 자르다[깎다]
This knife won't _____ . 이 칼은 잘 안 든다.

③ a _____ artist/hotel 유명한 화가/호텔
a _____ writer 유명한 작가

④ to _____ a question 질문을 반복하다
_____ the following words after me. 다음 말들을 따라 하시오.

⑤ the depths of the _____ 대양 깊은 곳[심해]
go swimming in the _____ 해수욕을 가다

⑥ an _____ job 사무직
a doctor's/dentist's _____ 의사/치과 의사 진료실

⑦ a _____-haired girl 빨간 머리의 소녀
She went _____ as a beetroot. 그녀는 얼굴이 홍당무가 되었다.

> **famous   look   repeat   Ocean   Red   office   Cut**

C 보기에 주어진 단어의 설명입니다. 해당되는 단어를 찾아 적으세요.

① (문제·곤경의) 해법, 해결책 _____

② 너무 (…한) _____

③ 조금, 약간의, 몇몇의 _____

④ 연장, 도구, 공구 _____

⑤ 군인, 병사 _____

⑥ 어조, 말투 _____

⑦ (말·글로) 알리다[전하다], 말하다 _____

| some | soldier | tell | solution | tool | tone | too |

D 주어진 해석에 맞는 영어단어로 퍼즐을 완성하세요.

Across

2. 농장, 농원
3. 밝은, 선명한
5. 군인, 병사
9. 지역, 지방
10. 해결하다

Down

1. 유명한
3. 다리
4. 심장, 가슴
6. 장소
7. 기억하다
8. 반복하다

A 주어진 문장에 맞는 단어를 보기에서 찾아 문장을 완성하세요.

① I _____ some flowers for you. 가져오다

② A rainy evening car _____ occurred. 사고

③ There are many _____ animals at night. 활동적인

④ The water is hot, be careful not to _____ yourself. 화상

⑤ Most children _____ a sandcastle. 짓다, 만들다

⑥ My _____ is a man of wisdom. 동생, 형, 오빠

⑦ I look good in _____ clothes. 갈색

⑧ You ought to _____ your age! 행동

⑨ From my childhood I wanted to be an _____. 배우

⑩ _____ two teaspoons of salt. 합하다, 첨가하다

actor   add   brought   active   burn   accident   brown   build   brother   act

B 해석을 보고 빈칸에 해당되는 단어를 보기에서 찾아 적으세요.

① Let's take a look at the _____ 피해 상황을 살펴봅시다.

   fire/smoke/bomb/storm _____ 화재/흡연/폭탄/폭풍 피해

② a _____ suit 검은색 정장

   It's getting dark every minute. 점점 어두워지고 있다.

③ a big _____ man/woman 몸집이 크고 뚱뚱한 남자/여자

   foods which are low in _____ 지방이 적은 식품

④ God the _____ 하느님 아버지

   a _____ to the poor 빈민의 아버지

⑤ _____! Keep Out! 위험해요! 비켜요!

   He is a _____. 그는 위험인물이다.

⑥ the world's _____ runner 세계에서 가장 빠른 주자

⑦ modern/classical _____ 현대/고전 무용

   The next _____ will be a waltz. 다음 춤은 왈츠입니다.

father   dark   fat   danger   fastest   damage   dance

C 보기에 주어진 단어의 설명입니다. 해당되는 단어를 찾아 적으세요.

① (높이위치 등이) 낮은 _____

② 돕다, 거들다 _____

③ (특히 가족친구에 대한) 사랑 _____

④ (소리가) 큰, 시끄러운 _____

⑤ (수양이) 많음, 다량, 다수 _____

⑥ 여기에[에서/로], 이리 _____

⑦ 무거운, 육중한 (반의어 light) _____

| here | loud | heavy | lot | low | help | love |

D 주어진 해석에 맞는 영어단어로 퍼즐을 완성하세요.

Across

2. 갈색
3. 춤, 무용
5. 자동차사고
7. 사랑
8. 호의, 친절
9. 돕다, 거들다

Down

1. 소리, 음
3. 손상, 피해
4. 아버지
6. 남쪽

101	**advantage** [ædvǽntidʒ]	몡 유리한 점, 이점, 강점	Basketball has an advantage for tall people. 농구는 키큰 사람에게 유리한 점이 있다.
102	**busy** [bízi]	혱 바쁜 동 ~바쁘다. ~매달리다	You have been busy! 당신 바쁘셨군요!
103	**dead** [ded]	혱 죽은	Dead fish floated over the water. 죽은 물고기가 물 위로 떠올랐다.
104	**feed** [fi:d]	동 밥을 먹이다.	Can you feed the dog? 강아지 먹이좀 주시겠어요?
105	**high** [hai]	혱 높은, 높이가 ~인 몡 최고(수준,수치)	She has always aimed high. 그녀는 항상 목표를 높이 잡는다.
106	**lucky** [lʌki]	혱 운이 좋은, 행운의	The lucky number this week is seven. 이번주 행운의 숫자는 7이다.
107	**one** [wʌn]	쉬 하나(의) 대 사람, 사물을 가리킬 때	No one can go back to yesterday. 어느 누구도 어제로 돌아갈 수 없다.
108	**right** [rait]	혱 (도덕적으로) 옳은, 올바른 혱 (틀리지 않고) 맞는, 정확한	You may well be right. 너가 맞을 거에요.
109	**special** [spéʃəl]	몡 특별한 것 혱 특수한 특별한	She's a very special friend. 그녀는 매우 특별한 친구이다.
110	**track** [træk]	몡 자국, 발자국, 길	The train to Busan boards on track 9. 부산으로 가는 기차는 9번 선로에서 탑승한다.

● 단어와 문장을 따라 쓰세요.

advantage

Basketball has an advantage for tall people.

busy

You have been busy!

dead

Dead fish floated over the water.

feed

Can you feed the dog?

high

She has always aimed high.

lucky

The lucky number this week is seven.

one

No one can go back to yesterday.

right

You may well be right.

special

She's a very special friend.

track

The train to Busan boards on track 9.

111	**advice** [ædváis]	몡 조언, 충고	Your advice has been a great help. 당신의 충고가 큰 도움이 되었다.
112	**but** [bət]	쩝 그러나 쩐 …외에	Nobody came but me. 나외에는 아무도 오지 않았다.
113	**dear** [diər]	쪵 ~ 사랑하는, ~ 소중한	I write to you, my dear. 사랑하는 당신에게 편지를 씁니다.
114	**feel** [fiːl]	똉 느끼다.	I feel ready to drop. 금방이라도 쓰러질 것 같다.
115	**hill** [hil]	몡 언덕, 경사로	The ball rolled quickly down the hill. 공이 언덕 아래로 빠르게 굴러 내려갔다.
116	**machine** [məʃíːn]	몡 기계	This machine is very simple to use. 이 기계는 사용이 간단하다.
117	**only** [óunli]	쪵 유일한, 오직 뿐 오직, 단지	This line is cash only. 이 줄은 현금만 받습니다.
118	**ring** [riŋ]	똉 울리다, 오다 몡 반지, 고리	I ordered a ring for her. 나는 그녀를 위해 반지를 주문했다.
119	**speech** [spiːtʃ]	몡 연설, 담화	The president's acceptance speech began. 대통령 수락 연설이 시작되었다.
120	**trade** [treɪd]	몡 거래, 교역, 무역	They were taught how to trade. 그들은 거래하는 법을 배웠다.

advice

Your advice has been a great help.

but

Nobody came but me.

dear

I write to you, my dear.

feel

I feel ready to drop.

hill

The ball rolled quickly down the hill.

machine

This machine is very simple to use.

only

This line is cash only.

ring

I ordered a ring for her.

speech

The president's acceptance speech began.

trade

They were taught how to trade.

121	**afraid** [əfréid]	형 두려워하는, 겁내는	Suddenly everything was afraid. 갑자기 모든 것이 두려워졌다.
122	**buy** [bai]	동 사다, 구입하다.	I went to the mart to buy a drink. 나는 마트에 음료를 사러 갔다.
123	**death** [deθ]	명 죽는 것, 죽음, 사망	His sudden death surprised everyone. 그의 갑작스런 죽음은 모두를 놀라게 했다.
124	**feet** [fiːt]	명 foot의 복수	My feet were icy cold. 나는 발이 얼음장 같았다.
125	**him** [hɪm]	대 그	I still hate him. 나는 아직도 그가 싫다.
126	**made** [meid]	명 make의 과거, 과거분사 동 만들다, 제조하다.	He's made a lot of new friends. 그는 새로운 친구를 많이 사귀었다.
127	**open** [óupən]	동 열다 형 열려있는	I pushed the door open. 나는 그 문을 밀어서 열었다.
128	**rise** [raiz]	명 인상, 증가 동 오르다, 올라가다	Prices continued to rise. 물가는 계속 올랐다.
129	**speed** [spiːd]	명 속도	The train began to run at high speed. 기차는 빠른 속도로 달리기 시작했다.
130	**train** [trein]	명 기차, 열차	I like traveling by train. 나는 기차 여행을 좋아한다.

단어와 문장을 따라 쓰세요.

afraid

Suddenly everything was afraid.

buy

I went to the mart to buy a drink.

death

His sudden death surprised everyone.

feet

My feet were icy cold.

him

I still hate him.

made

He's made a lot of new friends.

open

I pushed the door open.

rise

Prices continued to rise.

speed

The train began to run at high speed.

train

I like traveling by train.

131	**after** [ǽftər]	전 ~ 뒤에, ~ 후에 접 ~한 뒤[후]에	Water well after sowing. 씨를 뿌린 후에 물을 잘 주어야한다.
132	**by** [bai]	전 ··· 수단. 방법으로 부 (···을) 지나서	He comes to work by bus. 그는 버스를 타고 직장에 온다.
133	**debt** [det]	명 빚, 부채, 신세를 짐	The business failure caused debt. 사업 실패로 부채가 생겼다.
134	**fell** [fel]	통 넘어뜨리다.	He tripped and fell. 그는 발을 헛디며 넘어졌다.
135	**his** [hɪz]	대 그의 것, (그 사람) 자기(자신)의 것	His second book is better than his first. 그의 두번째 책이 그의 첫번째 책보다 좋다.
136	**magnet** [mǽgnit]	명 자석, ~을 끄는	This is a very strong magnet. 이 자석은 자력이 세다
137	**operate** [ápərèit]	통 작동하다, 가동하다.	I want to operate a cafe. 나는 카페를 운영하기 원한다.
138	**river** [rívər]	명 강	Can I swim in the river? 강에서 수영해도 될까요?
139	**spell** [spel]	통 철자를 맞게 쓰다 명 한동안 지속되는	How do you spell your surname? 당신 성의 철자를 어떻게 쓰나요?
140	**travel** [trǽvəl]	통 여행하다, 이동하다.	We always travel first class. 우리는 항상 1등석을 타고 다닌다.

after

Water well after sowing.

by

He comes to work by bus.

debt

The business failure caused debt.

fell

He tripped and fell.

his

His second book is better than his first.

magnet

This is a very strong magnet.

operate

I want to operate a cafe.

river

Can I swim in the river?

spell

How do you spell your surname?

travel

We always travel first class.

141	**again** [əgén]	튀 한 번 더, 다시 튀 그만큼 더	When will I see you again? 언제 다시 너를 만날 수 있을까?
142	**cable** [kéibl]	명 케이블, 전선	I applied for a local cable broadcast. 지역 유선 방송을 신청했다.
143	**decide** [disáid]	통 결정하다. 판결하다.	You choose, I can't decide. 네가 선택해, 나는 결정을 못하겠어.
144	**felt** [felt]	통 feel의 과거·과거분사 형 느껴지는	I felt a deep sadness. 나는 깊은 슬픔을 느꼈다.
145	**history** [hístəri]	명 역사	He is interested in history. 그는 역사에 관심이 많다.
146	**main** [mein]	형 가장큰	Where's the main post office? 중앙 우체국은 어디에 있죠?
147	**opinion** [əpínjən]	명 의견, 견해	I want to hear your honest opinion. 너의 솔직한 의견을 듣고 싶다.
148	**road** [roud]	명 도로, 길	We parked on a side road. 우리는 옆길에 주차 했습니다.
149	**spend** [spend]	통 돈을쓰다, 시간을보내다.	You spend too much time playing games. 게임을 하는데 많은 시간을 보낸다.
150	**tree** [tri:]	명 나무	I plucked an apple from the tree. 나는 그 나무에서 사과를 하나 땄다.

again

When will I see you again?

cable

I applied for a local cable broadcast.

decide

You choose, I can't decide.

felt

I felt a deep sadness.

history

He is interested in history.

main

Where's the main post office?

opinion

I want to hear your honest opinion.

road

We parked on a side road.

spend

You spend too much time playing games.

tree

I plucked an apple from the tree.

151	**against** [əgénst]	전 ~ 반대하여, ~ 가까이	She came out against the plan. 그녀는 그 계획을 반대하고 나섰다.
152	**call** [kɔːl]	동 ~라고 부르다. 명 전화	Can you call back tomorrow? 내일 다시 전화해 주시겠어요?
153	**deep** [diːp]	형 깊은 부 깊이, 깊은곳으로	deep in the forest. 숲속 깊은 곳으로
154	**few** [fjuː]	한 형용사 약간의, 적지 않은 대 소수, 적은 수	The letter came a few days ago. 그 편지는 며칠 전에 왔다.
155	**hit** [hit]	동 때리다, 부딪치다.	The ball flew off and hit him. 공이 날아가 그를 맞췄다.
156	**major** [méidʒər]	형 주요한, 중대한	A major mistake was found in the product. 제품에서 중대한 실수가 발견되었다.
157	**opposite** [ápəzit]	형 맞은편 ~ 다른편에	She sat down in the chair opposite. 그녀는 맞은편에 앉아 있었다.
158	**rock** [rak]	명 암석 동 흔들리다	The ship struck a rock. 그 배는 암초에 부딪쳤다.
159	**spoke** [spouk]	동 speak의 과거	She spoke in a loud voice. 그녀는 큰 소리로 말했다.
160	**triangle** [tráiæŋgl]	명 삼각형, 삼각관계	The child is drawing a triangle on the paper. 아이는 종이 위에 삼각형을 그리고 있다.

against
She came out against the plan.

call
Can you call back tomorrow?

deep
deep in the forest.

few
The letter came a few days ago.

hit
The ball flew off and hit him.

major
A major mistake was found in the product.

opposite
She sat down in the chair opposite.

rock
The ship struck a rock.

spoke
She spoke in a loud voice.

triangle
The child is drawing a triangle on the paper.

161	**age** [eɪdʒ]	명 나이, 연령, 수명	Age is only a number. 나이는 숫자에 불과하다.
162	**came** [keim]	통 come의 과거	We came by bus. 우리는 버스를 타고 왔다.
163	**depend** [dipénd]	자 의존하다, 의지하다	It really does depend on that. 이것은 정말로 그것에 달려있다.
164	**field** [fiːld]	명 들판	She walked across the field. 그녀는 들판을 가로질러 걸어갔다.
165	**hold** [hould]	통 잡다, 쥐다.	Can I hold your hand? 내가 너의 손을 잡아도 될까?
166	**make** [meik]	통 만들다(제품,문서등)	Would you make a photocopy? 사진 복사좀 해 주실래요?
167	**order** [ɔ́ːrdər]	명 순서, 정리 통 명령하다	Can I order? 주문해도 될까요?
168	**roll** [roul]	명 통, 두루마리 통 굴리다, 굴러가다	They roll dung into a ball. 그들은 똥을 굴려 공을 만든다.
169	**spread** [spred]	통 펼치다 명 확산	The light disappeared and the darkness spread. 빛이 사라지고 어둠이 번졌다.
170	**trip** [trip]	명 여행	What about a trip to London? 런던으로 여행가는거 어때?

age
Age is only a number.

came
We came by bus.

depend
It really does depend on that.

field
She walked across the field.

hold
Can I hold your hand?

make
Would you make a photocopy?

order
Can I order?

roll
They roll dung into a ball.

spread
The light disappeared and the darkness spread.

trip
What about a trip to London?

171	**ago** [əgóu]	🔊 ~ 전에	I saw Minho three days ago. 나는 민호를 3일전에 보았다.
172	**camp** [kæmp]	몡 야영지, 텐트	My son goes to an English camp during vacation. 나의 아들은 방학이면 영어 캠프를 간다.
173	**describe** [diskráib]	통 서술하다, 묘사하다.	Describe an accident moment. 사고 순간을 서술해 보세요.
174	**fight** [fait]	통 싸우다	They fight all the time for the sake of money. 그들은 돈때문에 항상 싸운다.
175	**hole** [houl]	몡 구덩이, 구멍	The golf ball went into the hole. 골프공이 구멍으로 들어갔다.
176	**man** [mæn]	몡 (성인) 남자 몡 사람들, 인류	He seems a nice man. 그는 좋은 사람인것 같다.
177	**original** [ərídʒənl]	혱 본래의, 원래의	This is a copy and the original is in the museum. 이것은 모조품이고 원본은 박물관에 있습니다.
178	**room** [ru:m]	몡 방	She looked about the room. 그녀는 방 구석구석을 보았다.
179	**spring** [spriŋ]	몡 봄, 스프링, 용수철	Spring came early this year. 올해는 봄이 일찍 왔다.
180	**trouble** [trʌbl]	몡 애, 문제, 곤란, 골칫거리	I'm just having trouble sleeping. 제대로 잠을 잘 못자요.

ago

I saw Minho three days ago.

camp

My son goes to an English camp during vacation.

describe

Describe an accident moment.

fight

They fight all the time for the sake of money.

hole

The golf ball went into the hole.

man

He seems a nice man.

original

This is a copy and the original is in the museum.

room

She looked about the room.

spring

Spring came early this year.

trouble

I'm just having trouble sleeping.

181	**agree** [əgríː]	동 의견이 일치하다, 합의가 되다	I couldn't agree with him. 나는 그의 말에 동의 할 수 없었다.
182	**campus** [kǽmpəs]	명 대학 교정, 캠퍼스	The university campus is so beautiful. 대학교 교정이 너무 아름답다.
183	**desert** [dézərt]	명 사막 동 버리다, 저버리다.	It is not easy to find water in the desert. 사막에서 물을 찾기는 쉽지 않다.
184	**figure** [fígjər]	명 수치, 숫자 명 모형장난감 동 중요하다.	Figure out how much it will cost. 가격이 얼마인지 계산해 주세요.
185	**holiday** [hálədèi]	명 휴가, 방학	This holiday goes to Jeju Island. 이번 휴일에는 제주도로 간다.
186	**manner** [mǽnər]	명 예의, 태도	She had a very easy manner. 그녀의 태도가 아주 좋았다.
187	**other** [ʌ́ðər]	형 (그 밖의) 다른, 다른 사람	Other times, other manners. 시대가 다르면 예절도 다르다.
188	**rope** [roup]	명 밧줄, 로프	You must take the rope when climbing. 등산할때 밧줄을 꼭 챙겨야 한다.
189	**square** [skwɛ́ər]	형 직각의, (거의) 직각을 이루는 광장	How can I get to Washington Square? 워싱턴 광장에 어떻게 가나요?
190	**truck** [trʌk]	명 트럭(차)	Heavy ones are carried by truck. 무거운 것들은 트럭으로 옮긴다.

agree

I couldn't agree with him.

campus

The university campus is so beautiful.

desert

It is not easy to find water in the desert.

figure

Figure out how much it will cost.

holiday

This holiday goes to Jeju Island.

manner

She had a very easy manner.

other

Other times, other manners.

rope

You must take the rope when climbing.

square

How can I get to Washington Square?

truck

Heavy ones are carried by truck.

191	**air** [er]	몡 공기, 대기	Let's air out the room. 실내 환기좀 시키자.
192	**can** [kən]	조 …할 수 있다. 할 줄 알다	I can do it. 나는 할 수 있다.
193	**design** [dizáin]	몡 디자인, 설계	The product is excellent in design. 그 제품은 디자인이 뛰어나다.
194	**fill** [fil]	동 채우다, 채워지다.	Fill in your full name and address. 성명과 주소를 적어 넣으세요.
195	**home** [houm]	몡 집, 주택 혱 집의, 가정의	I came home by taxi. 나는 택시를 타고 집으로 왔다.
196	**many** [méni]	한 몡 많은, 대부분	How many people were there? 그곳에 사람들이 얼마나 많았나요?
197	**our** [auər]	한 우리의, 저희의	Our victory was hard-won. 우리의 승리는 어렵게 얻은 것이다.
198	**rose** [rouz]	몡 장미 동 RISE의 과거	I planted rose trees in my house. 나는 집에 장미 나무를 심었다.
199	**stand** [stænd]	동 서다, 서 있다, 일어서다	They stand in line. 그들은 일렬로 서 있다.
200	**true** [tru:]	혱 사실의, 진짜, 정확한	The news cannot be true. 그 소식이 사실일리 없다.

air
Let's air out the room.

can
I can do it.

design
The product is excellent in design.

fill
Fill in your full name and address.

home
I came home by taxi.

many
How many people were there?

our
Our victory was hard-won.

rose
I planted rose trees in my house.

stand
They stand in line.

true
The news cannot be true.

A 주어진 문장에 맞는 단어를 보기에서 찾아 문장을 완성하세요.

1 Basketball has an _____ for tall people. 장점, 유리하다

2 You have been ( )! 바쁜

3 Your _____ has been a great help. 조언, 충고

4 Nobody came _____ me. ~외에

5 Suddenly everything was _____ 두려워하는, 겁내는

6 I went to the mart to _____ a drink. 사다, 구입하다

7 Water well _____ sowing. ~후에, 뒤에

8 He comes to work _____ bus. ~로

9 When will I see you _____? 다시

10 I applied for a local _____ broadcast. 케이블

> **again   after   afraid   advice   advantage   busy   cable   by   buy   but**

B 해석을 보고 빈칸에 해당되는 단어를 보기에서 찾아 적으세요.

1 It's up to you to _____. 결정은 너에게 달렸어

_____ a question 문제를 해결하다

2 a heavy _____ of snow 폭설이 내리다.

Apples _____ off the tree. 사과들이 나무에서 떨어진다.

3 One of the kids _____ into the river. 그 아이들 중 한 명이 강에 빠졌다.

His temperature _____. 그의 체온이 내려갔다.

4 _____ Sir or Madam 관계되시는 분께

Their baby's a _____ little thing. 그들의 아기는 너무 귀여워.

5 a _____ person/animal 죽은 사람/동물

_____ matches 다 탄 성냥

6 winter _____ for the horses 그 말들의 겨울용 사료

_____ a family 가족을 부양하다

7 a friend of _____ 그의 친구 한 명

He broke _____ leg skiing. 그는 스키를 타다가 다리가 부러졌다.

> **decide   his   dead   dear   feed   fall   fell**

C 보기에 주어진 단어의 설명입니다. 해당되는 단어를 찾아 적으세요.

① (재료를 섞거나 모아서) 만들다[제작/제조하다] _____

② (흔히 합성어에서) 기계 _____

③ (같은 종류 중) 가장 큰[중요한], 주된 _____

④ 자석, 자철 _____

⑤ (말이나 글로 기록된) 역사, 역사서, 역사물 _____

⑥ 운이 좋은, 행운의 (유의어 fortunate) _____

⑦ (사물의 바닥에서 꼭대기까지가) 높은 (반의어 low) _____

| high | history | make | machine | main | lucky | magnet |

D 주어진 해석에 맞는 영어단어로 퍼즐을 완성하세요.

Across

1. 의견, 견해
3. 기계
5. 여행하다
7. 연설, 담화
9. 속도

Down

2. 작동하다, 가동하다
4. 조언, 충고
6. 결정하다, 판결하다
8. 열다

A 주어진 문장에 맞는 단어를 보기에서 찾아 문장을 완성하세요.

❶ She came out _____ the plan. 반대하여

❷ Can you _____ back tomorrow? 전화, 통화

❸ _____ is only a number. 나이

❹ We _____ by bus. come의 과거, 왔다

❺ I saw Minho three days _____. 전에

❻ My son goes to English _____ during vacation. 방학동안 특별활동, 캠프

❼ I couldn't _____ with him. 동의

❽ The university _____ is so beautiful. (대학)교정

❾ Let's _____ out the room. 공기, 대기

❿ I _____ do it. 할 수 있다

age   camp   campus   against   call   agree   ago   air   can   came

B 해석을 보고 빈칸에 해당되는 단어를 보기에서 찾아 적으세요.

❶ a man of _____ words 말수가 적은 사람

He has _____ friends. 그에게는 친구가 거의 없다.

❷ a _____ studio 디자인[설계]실

_____ an attack 공격을 계획하다.

❸ soldiers trained to _____ 전투 훈련을 받은 군인들

a street/gang _____ 길거리 싸움/패싸움

❹ a _____ of wheat 밀밭

a sports _____ 운동 경기장

❺ the Sahara _____ 사하라 사막

Somalia is mostly _____. 소말리아는 대부분이 사막이다.

❻ I _____ on your word. 나는 네 말을 믿는다.

❼ a _____ hole/well/river 깊은 구멍/우물/강

a _____ cut/wound 깊게 베인 상처/깊은 상처

design   field   deep   depend   few   fight   desert

C 보기에 주어진 단어의 설명입니다. 해당되는 단어를 찾아 적으세요.

1 (손팔 등으로) 잡고[쥐고/들고/안고/받치고] 있다. _____

2 (격식) (일의) 방식 _____

3 (재료를 섞거나 모아서) 만들다. _____

4 (손이나 손에 들고 있는 물건으로) 때리다. _____

5 (직장의) 휴가, 방학 _____

6 [명사] 구멍 , [동사] (특히 보트나 배에) 구멍을 내다. _____

7 (주로 명사 앞에 씀) 주요한, 중대한 _____

| hit | hole | manner | hold | major | holiday | make |

D 주어진 해석에 맞는 영어단어로 퍼즐을 완성하세요.

Across
2. 휴가, 방학
6. 문제, 곤란
7. 삼각형
8. 순서, 명령하다
10. 주요한, 중대한

Down
1. 잡다, 쥐다
3. 서술하다, 묘사하다
4. 본래의, 원래의
5. 사망
9. 트럭(차)

201	**airline** [eˈrlai]	명 항공사	The airline failed to depart due to a strike. 항공사의 파업으로 출발하지 못했다.
202	**capital** [kǽpətl]	명 수도	The capital of Egypt? 이집트의 수도는?
203	**desk** [desk]	명 책상, 데스크	He was sitting at her desk. 그는 책상에 앉아 있었다.
204	**final** [fáinl]	형 마지막, 최종적인	It's up to you to make the final decision. 최종 결정은 너에게 달려있다.
205	**hope** [houp]	동 바라다, 희망[기대]하다	I hope you have a safe journey. 안전한 여행이 되길 바란다.
206	**map** [mæp]	명 지도, 약도	He was looking at a map. 그는 지도를 보고 있었다.
207	**out** [aut]	부, 전 집에 있지 않은, 자리에 없는	The boats are all out at sea. 그 배들은 모두 바다에 나가있다.
208	**round** [raund]	형 둥근, 동그란 부 둥글게, 빙빙	The shape of the room was round. 그 방은 둥근 모양이었다.
209	**star** [staːr]	명 별, 항성 동 주연을 맡다	She was once the most popular movie star. 그녀는 한때 유명한 영화배우였다.
210	**try** [trai]	동 노력하다 명 시도	You must try harder. 더 열심히 노력해야한다.

단어와 문장을 따라 쓰세요.

airline
The airline failed to depart due to a strike.

capital
The capital of Egypt?

desk
He was sitting at her desk.

final
It's up to you to make the final decision.

hope
I hope you have a safe journey.

map
He was looking at a map.

out
The boats are all out at sea.

round
The shape of the room was round.

star
She was once the most popular movie star.

try
You must try harder.

211	**airport** [eˈrpɔˌrt]	명 공항	We arrived at the airport not too late. 우리는 공항에 늦지 않게 도착했다.
212	**captain** [kǽptən]	명 선장, 기장, 주장	The captain lifted the trophy. 주장이 트로피를 들어 올렸다.
213	**develop** [divéləp]	통 성장하다, 개발하다.	It is important to develop good study skills. 훌륭한 학습법을 개발하는 것이 중요하다.
214	**find** [faind]	통 찾다, 발견하다	Can you find me my bag? 내 가방 좀 찾아주겠니?
215	**horse** [hɔːrs]	명 말	The woman is riding a horse. 여자가 말을 타고 있다.
216	**mark** [maːrk]	통 표시하다. 흔적이 나다. 명 흔적	There's a mark on your skirt. 네 치마에 얼룩이 있다.
217	**outcome** [auˈtkə]	명 결과	This is the outcome. 이런 결과가 나왔다.
218	**row** [rou]	명 열, 줄	Just won eight in a row. 방금 8연승 했다.
219	**start** [staːrt]	통 시작하다. 명 시작	Can you start on Sunday? 일요일부터 시작할 수 있겠어?
220	**tube** [tjuːb]	명 튜브, 관	The British subway is called a tube. 영국의 지하철을 튜브라고 부른다.

airport

We arrived at the airport not too late.

captain

The captain lifted the trophy.

develop

It is important to develop good study skills.

find

Can you find me my bag?

horse

The woman is riding a horse.

mark

There's a mark on your skirt.

outcome

This is the outcome.

row

Just won eight in a row.

start

Can you start on Sunday?

tube

The British subway is called a tube.

221	**album** [ǽlbəm]	몡 앨범(음악, 사진)	There are many good songs on the new album. 새 앨범에는 좋은 노래들이 많다.
222	**car** [ka:r]	몡 승용차, 차	Always lock your car. 항상 차문을 잠가라.
223	**dictionary** [díkʃənèri]	몡 사전	I found a word in the dictionary I didn't know. 나는 모르는 단어를 사전에서 찾았다.
224	**fine** [fain]	혱 질 높은, 좋은	This machine works fine. 이 기계는 작동이 잘 된다.
225	**hot** [hat]	혱 더운 혱 (더위를 느끼게 하는) 뜨거운	Seoul was hot and dusty. 서울은 덥고 먼지가 많았다.
226	**market** [má:rkit]	몡 시장	The traditional market is cheap. 전통 시장이 가격이 싸다.
227	**over** [óuvər]	붱 넘어지게, 쓰러지게 젠 ~위에	She lives over the road. 그녀는 도로 반대편에 산다.
228	**rule** [ru:l]	몡 원칙, 규칙 동 다스리다, 지배하다	We must all follow a simple rule. 우리는 간단한 규칙을 지켜야 합니다.
229	**state** [steɪt]	몡 상태, 국가, 나라	I'm in a state of shock. 나는 충격을 받은 상태이다.
230	**turn** [tə:rn]	동 돌다, 돌리다, 돌라서다.	Please turn the volume down. 소리좀 낮춰 주시겠어요.

● 단어와 문장을 따라 쓰세요.

album

There are many good songs on the new album.

car

Always lock your car.

dictionary

I found a word in the dictionary I didn't know.

fine

This machine works fine.

hot

Seoul was hot and dusty.

market

The traditional market is cheap.

over

She lives over the road.

rule

We must all follow a simple rule.

state

I'm in a state of shock.

turn

Please turn the volume down.

231	**alive** [əláiv]	혱 살아있는	I believe he is alive. 나는 그가 살아 있다고 믿는다.
232	**card** [kaːrd]	몡 카드	Credit card usage has increased over cash. 현금보다 신용카드 사용이 늘었다.
233	**die** [daɪ]	동 죽다, 사망하다	Many people die in car accidents. 자동차 사고로 많은 사람이 죽는다.
234	**finger** [fíŋgər]	몡 손가락	He cut his finger on a piece of glass. 그는 유리 조각에 손가락을 베었다.
235	**hour** [auər]	몡 시간	She's been gone an hour. 그녀가 떠난지 한 시간이 되었다.
236	**mass** [mæs]	혱 대량의, 대규모의, 대중적인 몡 많은	The room was a mass of trash. 방에 쓰레기 투성이었다.
237	**own** [oun]	때, 혱 ~ 자신의	Is the car your own? 그 차가 당신 차인가요?
238	**run** [rʌn]	동 달리다, 뛰다. 몡 달리기	I can run fast. 나는 빨리 달릴 수 있다.
239	**station** [stéiʃən]	몡 역, 정거장	You have to get off this station and take a bus. 이번 역에서 내려 버스로 갈아타야 한다.
240	**twenty** [twénti]	쉬 20, 스물 몡 20대	She was taken off after twenty minutes. 그녀는 20분 후에 떠나야 했다.

alive
I believe he is alive.

card
Credit card usage has increased over cash.

die
Many people die in car accidents.

finger
He cut his finger on a piece of glass.

hour
She's been gone an hour.

mass
The room was a mass of trash.

own
Is the car your own?

run
I can run fast.

station
You have to get off this station and take a bus.

twenty
She was taken off after twenty minutes.

241	**all** [ɔːl]	한 모든 대 다, 모두	All aboard! 모두 타세요!
242	**care** [kɛər]	명 돌봄, 보살핌, 주의	Take care, my love. 조심해, 내 사랑.
243	**differ** [dífər]	동 의견이 다르다, 동의하지 않다	I agree to differ. 나는 네 의견에 동의하지 않아.
244	**finish** [fíniʃ]	동 끝내다, 마무리하다.	I have to finish my homework by nine. 나는 아홉시까지 숙제를 끝내야 한다.
245	**house** [haus]	명 집, 주택 동 살 곳을 주다	The house is in good repair. 그집은 수리가 잘되어있다.
246	**master** [mǽstər]	동 ~완전히 익히다, ~에 숙달하다 명 주인	The shoes were made by the Italian master. 이 구두는 이태리 장인에 의해 만들어졌다.
247	**oxygen** [áksidʒen]	명 산소	In space, there is a lack of oxygen. 우주에서는 산소가 부족하다.
248	**safe** [seif]	형 안전한, 안심할 수 있는	Thank God you're safe! 네가 안전해서 정말 다행이다!
249	**stay** [stei]	동 그대로 있다. 계속있다. 명 머무름, 방문	Stay as long as you like. 있고 싶은데로 머물러 있어.
250	**type** [taip]	명 유형, 종류, 사람, 타입	What is your blood type? 당신의 혈액형은 무엇입니까?

all

All aboard!

care

Take care, my love.

differ

I agree to differ.

finish

I have to finish my homework by nine.

house

The house is in good repair.

master

The shoes were made by the Italian master.

oxygen

In space, there is a lack of oxygen.

safe

Thank God you're safe!

stay

Stay as long as you like.

type

What is your blood type?

251	**allow** [əláu]	동 허락하다, 용납하다.	They don't allow smoking indoors. 실내에서 흡연은 허용되지 않습니다.
252	**careful** [kɛ́ərfəl]	형 조심하는, 주의 깊은	Be careful when you cross the street. 길을 건널 때 조심해야한다.
253	**difficult** ['dɪfɪkəlt]	형 어려운, 힘든	Math problems are always difficult. 수학 문제는 항상 어렵다.
254	**fire** [faiər]	명 불, 화재	Most animals are afraid of fire. 동물 대부분은 불을 무서워한다.
255	**how** [hau]	부 어떻게	How are you? 어떻게 지내니?
256	**match** [mætʃ]	명 경기, 시합 명 성냥	This is a very important match. 이것은 매우 중요한 경기이다.
257	**package** [pǽkidʒ]	명 포장 동 포장하다	A large package arrived. 큰 소포가 도착했다.
258	**said** [sed]	동 말하다, …라고 (말)하다	I didn't believe a word he said. 나는 그가 하는 말을 한마디도 믿지 않았다.
259	**stead** [sted]	명 대신, 대리, 위함, 유용, 쓸모 타 ~ 도움이 되다.	Let me apologize in her stead. 그녀는 대신해 제가 사과할께요.
260	**under** [ʌndər]	전 ~아래에 부 ~ 속으로	He dived under the water. 그는 수면 아래로 잠수해 들어갔다.

allow

They don't allow smoking indoors.

careful

Be careful when you cross the street.

difficult

Math problems are always difficult.

fire

Most animals are afraid of fire.

how

How are you?

match

This is a very important match.

package

A large package arrived.

said

I didn't believe a word he said.

stead

Let me apologize in her stead.

under

He dived under the water.

261	**also** [ɔ́:lsou]	🖲 또한, 게다가, …도	It is also very inexpensive. 가격또한 매우 저렴하다.
262	**carry** [kǽri]	🖲 휴대하다, 가지고 있다.	He is able to carry this bag. 그는 이 가방을 들 수 있다.
263	**direct** [dirékt]	🖲 직접적인 🖲 ~로 향하다.	Is this a direct line? 직통 전화인가요?
264	**first** [fə:rst]	🖲 첫째 🖲 우선, 먼저	When did you first meet him? 당신은 언제 그를 처음 만났나요?
265	**huge** [hju:dʒ]	🖲 거대한, 성공한	A huge wave came. 거대한 파도가 밀려왔다.
266	**material** [mətíəriəl]	🖲 직물, 천 🖲 물질적인	This material is soft. 이 옷감은 부드럽다.
267	**page** [peidʒ]	🖲 페이지, 쪽, 면	They're just reading the sports page. 그 사람들은 스포츠 기사만 읽고 있다.
268	**sail** [seil]	🖲 항해를 하다. 요트를 타다.	Submarines sail under the water. 잠수함은 물 밑을 다닌다.
269	**steam** [sti:m]	🖲 증기, 김	There is a steam-powered train. 증기 기관차가 있다.
270	**unit** [jú:nit]	🖲 단위, 구성	The family is the smallest unit of society. 가족은 사회의 가장 작은 구성 단위이다.

단어와 문장을 따라 쓰세요.

also

It is also very inexpensive.

carry

He is able to carry this bag.

direct

Is this a direct line?

first

When did you first meet him?

huge

A huge wave came.

material

This material is soft.

page

They're just reading the sports page.

sail

Submarines sail under the water.

steam

There is a steam-powered train.

unit

The family is the smallest unit of society.

271	**always** [ɔ́:lweiz]	閉 항상, 언제나	He always gets up early. 그는 항상 일찍 일어난다.
272	**case** [keis]	명 사례, 경우, 사건, 사실	In this case, we follow custom. 이런 경우, 우리는 관례에 따른다.
273	**discovery** [diskΛvəri]	명 발견	The discovery of a new continent also began with curiosity. 새로운 대륙의 발견도 호기심에서 시작됐다.
274	**fish** [fiʃ]	명 물고기, 어류 동 낚시하다.	The lakes abound with fish. 그 호수에는 물고기가 많다.
275	**human** [hjú:mən]	형 인간적인, 인간이기에 갖게 되는	Human nature does not change. 인간의 본성은 변하지 않는다.
276	**matter** [mǽtər]	명 상황, 사태, 사정	Time will solve the matter. 그 문제는 시간이 해결해 줄 것이다.
277	**paint** [peint]	명 그림물감, 페인트	It's fun to paint. 그림을 그리니 재미있다.
278	**salt** [sɔːlt]	명 소금	Eating a lot of salt is bad for your body. 소금을 많이 먹으면 몸에 좋지 않다.
279	**steel** [stiːl]	명 강철, 강철업	Pohang Steel is a very large company. 포항 제철은 아주 큰 기업이다.
280	**until** [əntíl]	전 ~ 때까지	I will stay there until July 3rd. 나는 7월 3일까지 그곳에 있을 것이다.

always
He always gets up early.

case
In this case, we follow custom.

discovery
The discovery of a new continent also began with curiosity.

fish
The lakes abound with fish.

human
Human nature does not change.

matter
Time will solve the matter.

paint
It's fun to paint.

salt
Eating a lot of salt is bad for your body.

steel
Pohang Steel is a very large company.

until
I will stay there until July 3rd.

281	**among** [əmʌŋ]	젠 ~ 중에, ~ 둘러싸인, ~ 가운데	I include you among my friends. 나는 너를 친구중 한 사람으로 생각하고 있다.
282	**cat** [kæt]	명 고양이	The cat tries to catch a mouse. 고양이가 쥐를 잡으려고 해요.
283	**discuss** [diskʌs]	동 상의하다, 논의하다.	He is not entitled to discuss. 그는 토론할 자격이 없다.
284	**fishing** [fíʃiŋ]	명 낚시	I go fishing every weekend. 주말마다 낚시를 간다.
285	**hundred** [hʌndrəd]	수 100 백	I've used it a hundred times. 나는 그것을 백번 사용했다.
286	**may** [mei]	조 ~일지도 모른다	You may do as you like. 네가 하고 싶은대로 해도 된다.
287	**pair** [pɛər]	동 짝을 마추다 명 (같은 물건이 두개있 는) 짝	I need to get a new pair of glasses. 나는 새로운 안경이 필요하다.
288	**same** [seim]	형 같은, 동일한	We were in the same class at school. 우리는 같은 학교 동창이다.
289	**step** [step]	명 걸음, 걸음거리	He moved a step closer to me. 그가 내게로 한 걸음 더 가까이 다가왔다.
290	**up** [ʌp]	젠 위로, 위쪽으로 부 (윗쪽 방향) 다, 완전히	It's up to you. 너의 결정에 달렸어.

단어와 문장을 따라 쓰세요.

among

I include you among my friends.

cat

The cat tries to catch a mouse.

discuss

He is not entitled to discuss.

fishing

I go fishing every weekend.

hundred

I've used it a hundred times.

may

You may do as you like.

pair

I need to get a new pair of glasses.

same

We were in the same class at school.

step

He moved a step closer to me.

up

It's up to you.

291	**anger** [ǽŋgər]	몡 화, 분노	She screamed in anger. 그녀는 화가 나서 소리를 질렀다.
292	**catch** [kætʃ]	툉 잡다, 붙잡다	I have a plane to catch at 4 p.m. 나는 오후 4시에 비행기를 타야한다.
293	**dish** [diʃ]	몡 요리, 접시	Please bring the main dish quickly. 메인 요리를 빨리 가져다 주세요.
294	**fit** [fit]	툉 맞다. 혱 적합하다, 꼭 맞다.	The clothes fit my body. 옷이 내 몸에 딱 맞는다.
295	**hunt** [hʌnt]	툉 사냥하다, 찾다	Some animals hunt at night. 어떤 동물들은 밤에 사냥한다.
296	**me** [mi]	때 나를, 나에게	Call me a taxi. 택시를 좀 불러주세요.
297	**paper** [péipər]	몡 종이, 신문	Give me a piece of paper. 종이 한 장만 주세요.
298	**sand** [sænd]	몡 모래, 모래사장	They painted on the sand. 그들은 모래위에 그림을 그렸다.
299	**stick** [stik]	툉 붙이다, 박이다 몡 막대, 나뭇가지	The dog grabbed the stick with its mouth. 개가 입으로 막대기를 집었다.
300	**us** [əs]	때 우리 때 나를, 나에게	God have mercy on us. 신이여 우리를 불쌍히 여기소서.

anger
She screamed in anger.

catch
I have a plane to catch at 4 p. m.

dish
Please bring the main dish quickly.

fit
The clothes fit my body.

hunt
Some animals hunt at night.

me
Call me a taxi.

paper
Give me a piece of paper.

sand
They painted on the sand.

stick
The dog grabbed the stick with its mouth.

us
God have mercy on us.

A 주어진 문장에 맞는 단어를 보기에서 찾아 문장을 완성하세요.

❶ The _____ failed to depart due to a strike. 항공사

❷ The _____ of Egypt? 수도

❸ We arrived at the _____ not too late. 공항

❹ The _____ lifted the trophy. 주장(운동 팀)

❺ There are many good songs on the new _____. 앨범

❻ Always lock your _____. 자동차

❼ I believe he is _____. 살아있는

❽ Credit _____ usage has increased over cash. 카드

❾ _____ aboard! 다, 모두

❿ Take _____, my love. 조심, 주의

> care   card   car   captain   capital   airline   all   alive   airport   album

B 해석을 보고 빈칸에 해당되는 단어를 보기에서 찾아 적으세요.

❶ _____ a coin on the street 길에서 동전을 발견하다.

   _____ the lost key 잃어버린 열쇠를 찾아내다

❷ I beg to _____. 실례지만 나의 의견은 다릅니다.

   French and English _____ in this respect. 프랑스어와 영어는 이 점이 다르다.

❸ a Korean-English _____ 한영사전

❹ the _____ product 최종 산출물

   a _____ judgment 최종 판결

❺ the little _____ 새끼손가락

   _____ papers 서류를 만지작거리다.

❻ the check-in _____ 투숙객 접수처

   the sports _____ 스포츠 데스크

❼ _____ up the work 일을 끝내다

   _____ school 학업을 마치다

> find   dictionary   differ   finish   desk   final   finger

C 보기에 주어진 단어의 설명입니다. 해당되는 단어를 찾아 적으세요.

❶ ~바라다, 희망[기대]하다 _____

❷ (일반적인) 시장 _____

❸ ~ B on A (표기호 등으로) 표시하다 _____

❹ (흔히 하인종의) 주인 _____

❺ (날씨기온온도가) 더운[뜨거운] _____

❻ (특히 로마 가톨릭교에서) 미사 _____

❼ 집, 주택, 가옥 _____

| mass | master | mark | house | hot | market | hope |

D 주어진 해석에 맞는 영어단어로 퍼즐을 완성하세요.

Across

3. 수도
5. 돌다, 돌리다
6. 시장
8. 역, 정거장

Down

1. 결과
2. 손가락
4. 공항
7. 집

A 주어진 문장에 맞는 단어를 보기에서 찾아 문장을 완성하세요.

① They don't _____ smoking indoors. 허락, 허용

② Be _____ when you cross the street. 조심, 주의

③ It is _____ very inexpensive. 또한

④ He is able to _____ this bag. 휴대하다, 나르다

⑤ He _____ gets up early. 항상, 언제나

⑥ In this _____, we follow custom. 경우

⑦ I include you _____ my friends. ~중에서

⑧ The _____ tries to catch a mouse. 고양이

⑨ She screamed in _____. 화, 분노

⑩ I have a plane to _____ at 4 p.m. 잡다, 붙잡다

anger   catch   allow   carry   careful   always   also   among   cat   case

B 해석을 보고 빈칸에 해당되는 단어를 보기에서 찾아 적으세요.

① a _____ flight 직항 비행기

   a _____ hit 직통으로 맞음

② a _____ problem/task/exam 어려운 문제/과제/시험

③ to make/build a _____ 불을 피우다

   a log/coal _____ 장작불/석탄불

④ your _____ impressions 당신의 첫 인상

   the _____ of May / May 1st 5월 1일

⑤ tropical/marine/freshwater _____ 열대어/해양어류/민물고기

   take _____ in a net 그물로 물고기를 잡다

⑥ deep-sea _____ 원양 어업

   _____ grounds 어장

⑦ an oven proof _____ 오븐 사용 가능 접시

   a baking / serving _____ 오븐 구이용/음식 차림용 접시

dish   fishing   fish   fire   difficult   first   direct

C 보기에 주어진 단어의 설명입니다. 해당되는 단어를 찾아 적으세요.

① 직물, 천 (유의어 fabric) _____

② …일지도 모른다[…일 수도 있다] _____

③ 인간[사람]의 _____

④ (크기·양·정도가) 막대한[엄청난], 거대한 (유의어 enormous, vast) _____

⑤ 사냥하다 _____

⑥ (고려하거나 처리해야 할) 문제[일/사안] _____

⑦ 성냥, (특히 영국) 경기, 시합 _____

| huge | human | match | matter | may | hunt | material |

D 주어진 해석에 맞는 영어단어로 퍼즐을 완성하세요.

Across

3. 잡다, 붙잡다
4. 발견
5. 상의하다, 논의하다
7. 강철
8. 증기, 김

Down

1. 조심하는
2. ~아래에
5. 직접적인
6. 같은, 동일한

301	**animal** [ǽnəməl]	명 (식물과 인간을 제외한) 동물 형 동물적	A Tiger is a dangerous animal. 호랑이는 위험한 동물이다.
302	**caught** [kɔːt]	통 catch의 과거, 과거분사	I caught some fish by fishing. 낚시로 물고기 몇마리를 잡았다.
303	**display** [displéi]	명 전시, 진열 통 전시하다.	These cameras are for display. 이 카메라들은 전시용입니다.
304	**flat** [flæt]	형 평평한, 평지인 명 (주거형태) 플랫	I put the thing down on a flat floor. 평평한 바닥에 물건을 내려 놓았다.
305	**hurry** [hə́ːri]	통 서두르다, 급히 하다	If you hurry, you will not be late for your appointment. 서두르면 약속 시간에 늦지 않을 것이다.
306	**mean** [miːn]	통 ~라는 뜻이다, ~을 뜻하다	I know what you mean. 나는 무슨말인지 알겠다.
307	**parent** [pɛ́ərənt]	명 부모	Being a parent is a great joy. 부모가 되는 것은 큰 기쁨이다.
308	**sat** [sæt]	통 sit의 과거, 과거분사	We sat in gloomy silence. 우리는 말없이 침울하게 앉아 있었다.
309	**still** [stil]	부 아직, 그런데도 형 가만히 있는	I'm still hungry! 나는 아직까지 배고프다.
310	**use** [juːz]	통 쓰다, 사용하다 명 사용, 이용	Could I use your phone, please? 전화 좀 써도 될까요?

● 단어와 문장을 따라 쓰세요.

animal
A Tiger is a dangerous animal.

caught
I caught some fish by fishing.

display
These cameras are for display.

flat
I put the thing down on a flat floor.

hurry
If you hurry, you will not be late for your appointment.

mean
I know what you mean.

parent
Being a parent is a great joy.

sat
We sat in gloomy silence.

still
I'm still hungry!

use
Could I use your phone, please?

311	**answer** [ǽnsər]	명 대답, 회신, 대응 동 대답하다. 대응하다	Your answer is exactly right. 너의 대답이 정답이다.
312	**cause** [kɔːz]	명 원인, 이유	What was the cause of the fire? 그 화재의 원인은 무엇이죠?
313	**distant** [dístənt]	형 먼, 떨어져 있는	I feel so distant from him. 그가 멀리 느껴진다.
314	**floor** [flɔːr]	명 바닥	Do not spit on the floor. 바닥에 침을 뱉지 마세요.
315	**hurt** [həːrt]	동 아프다, 다치다.	He hurt his back while riding a bicycle. 그는 자전거를 타다가 허리를 다쳤다.
316	**meant** [ment]	동 mean의 과거, 과거분사	I don't know what you mean. 나는 너의 뜻을 잘 모르겠다.
317	**part** [paːrt]	명 일부, 약간, 부분 동 헤어지다	It is part of an art project. 이것은 미술 프로젝트의 일부이다.
318	**save** [seiv]	동 구하다, 저축하다.	We should save water. 우리는 물을 절약해야 한다.
319	**stone** [stoun]	명 돌, 돌맹이	I was hit by a stone he threw. 나는 그가 던진 돌에 맞았다.
320	**usual** [júːʒuəl]	형 흔히 하는, 보통의	My mother is as healthy as usual. 나의 어머니는 여전히 건강하시다.

answer
Your answer is exactly right.

cause
What was the cause of the fire?

distant
I feel so distant from him.

floor
Do not spit on the floor.

hurt
He hurt his back while riding a bicycle.

meant
I don't know what you mean.

part
It is part of an art project.

save
We should save water.

stone
I was hit by a stone he threw.

usual
My mother is as healthy as usual.

321	**any** [əni]	한 어느, 어떤 대 아무(것)	I didn't eat any meat. 나는 고기를 한 점도 안먹었다.
322	**cell** [sel]	명 세포 명 휴대폰	He was a cell phone salesman. 그는 휴대전화 판매원이었다.
323	**divide** [diváid]	동 나뉘다, 나누다.	Let's divide teams. 팀을 나누자.
324	**flow** [flou]	명 흐름 공급 동 흐르다	Traffic flow is smooth today. 오늘은 교통 흐름이 원활하다.
325	**ice** [ais]	명 얼음, 얼음판	She slipped on the ice. 그녀는 얼음판에서 미끄러 넘어졌다.
326	**meat** [mi:t]	명 고기	I prefer fish to meat. 나는 고기보다 생선을 더 좋아한다.
327	**party** [pá:rti]	명 정당, 파티	This is a party for all students. 모든 학생이 참가하는 파티입니다.
328	**saw** [sɔ:]	동 See의 과거	I saw him this morning. 나는 그를 오늘 아침에 봤다.
329	**stood** [stud]	동 stand의 과거, 과거분사	The children stood in a circle. 아이들이 동그랗게 모여 서 있었다.
330	**valley** [væli]	명 계곡, 골짜기	The valley is very rough. 그 계곡은 매우 험난하다.

● 단어와 문장을 따라 쓰세요.

any

I didn't eat any meat.

cell

He was a cell phone salesman.

divide

Let's divide teams.

flow

Traffic flow is smooth today.

ice

She slipped on the ice.

meat

I prefer fish to meat.

party

This is a party for all students.

saw

I saw him this morning.

stood

The children stood in a circle.

valley

The valley is very rough.

331	**anybody** [énibàdi]	때 누구든지, 아무나	Is anybody there? 거기 아무나 없나요?
332	**center** [séntər]	명 중앙, 한가운데	We wanted a town youth center. 우리 마을은 청년문화센터를 원했다.
333	**division** [divíʒən]	명 나눗셈, 나누기, 분할	The microscopy confirmed the cell division. 현미경을 통해 세포 분열을 확인했다.
334	**flower** [fláuər]	명 꽃 화초	They normally flower in the spring. 꽃들은 보통 봄에 핀다.
335	**idea** [aidíːə]	명 생각, 견해, 신념	What a clever idea! 재치있는 생각이다!
336	**meet** [miːt]	동 만나다.	We meet every Wednesday. 우리는 매주 수요일에 만난다.
337	**pass** [pæs]	동 지나가다, 통과하다	The school has 80% pass rate. 그 학교는 합격률이 80%이다.
338	**say** [sei]	동 ~라고 말하다, 말하다. 명 발언권	I cannot say. 나는 뭐라고 말할 수가 없다.
339	**stop** [stap]	동 멈추다, 그만두다.	I get off at the next stop. 나는 다음 정거장에서 내린다.
340	**value** [vǽljuː]	명 가치 동 소중하게 생각하다	You can't translate your value into money. 너의 가치를 돈으로 환산할 수 없다.

anybody
Is anybody there?

center
We wanted a town youth center.

division
The microscopy confirmed the cell division.

flower
They normally flower in the spring.

idea
What a clever idea!

meet
We meet every Wednesday.

pass
The school has 80% pass rate.

say
I cannot say.

stop
I get off at the next stop.

value
You can't translate your value into money.

341	**appear** [əpíər]	통 나타나다, 보이기 시작하다	When will the stars appear? 언제 별이 보이기 시작할까요?
342	**century** [séntʃəri]	명 세기, 100년	The house was built in the 16th century. 그 집은 16세기때 만들어 졌다.
343	**do** [du]	통 (동작이나 행위를) 하다 조 다른 동사 앞에 쓰여 부정문이나 의문문을 만듦	What do you want to do tomorrow? 내일은 무엇을 하고 싶니?
344	**fly** [flai]	통 날다, 비행하다.	He's learning to fly. 그는 조종비행을 배우고 있다.
345	**if** [if]	접 만약, …면, ~하기만하면	If I had only known! 만약 내가 그것을 알고만 있었더라면!
346	**melody** [mélədi]	명 멜로디, 곡	The song has a simple melody. 그 노래는 단조로운 곡으로 되어있다.
347	**passenger** [pǽsəndʒər]	명 승객	The passenger took another plane. 그 승객은 다른 비행기를 탔다.
348	**scale** [skeil]	명 규모, 등급 통 오르다	This event is small in scale. 이 행사는 규모가 작다.
349	**store** [stɔːr]	명 가게, 백화점	The store is having a sale. 그 상점은 세일을 하고 있다.
350	**vary** [vɛ́əri]	통 다르다, 달라지다.	Rates vary by day. 요금은 날짜에 따라 달라진다.

단어와 문장을 따라 쓰세요.

appear
When will the stars appear?

century
The house was built in the 16th century.

do
What do you want to do tomorrow?

fly
He's learning to fly.

if
If I had only known!

melody
The song has a simple melody.

passenger
The passenger took another plane.

scale
This event is small in scale.

store
The store is having a sale.

vary
Rates vary by day.

351	**apple** [ǽpl]	몡 사과	He peeled and quartered an apple. 그는 사과를 벗겨 4등분했다.
352	**certain** [sə́:rtn]	혱 확실한, 틀림없는	He looks certain to win an Oscar. 그는 오스카상을 탈 것이 확실해 보인다.
353	**doctor** [dáktər]	몡 의사	I want to be a good doctor. 나는 훌륭한 의사가 되고 싶다.
354	**follow** [fálou]	통 ~의 뒤를 따라가다, 따라오다. 통 뒤따르다	Follow me please. 저를 따라오세요.
355	**imagine** [imǽdʒin]	통 상상하다, 그리다.	I imagine winning the lottery. 나는 복권에 당첨되는 상상을 한다.
356	**metal** [métl]	몡 금속	This sword is made of metal. 이 검은 금속으로 만들어져 있다.
357	**past** [pæst]	혱 지나간, 지난	It happened in the past. 그 일은 과거에 있었다
358	**school** [sku:l]	몡 학교	I was good at sums at school. 나는 학교 다닐때 수학을 잘했다.
359	**story** ['stɔːri]	몡 이야기, 일대기, 역사	She read us a story. 그녀는 우리에게 이야기를 하나 읽어주었다.
360	**very** [véri]	뷔 매우, 아주, 정말 혱 바로	It was very hot in Seoul today. 오늘 서울은 무척 더웠다.

apple

He peeled and quartered an apple.

certain

He looks certain to win an Oscar.

doctor

I want to be a good doctor.

follow

Follow me please.

imagine

I imagine winning the lottery.

metal

This sword is made of metal.

past

It happened in the past.

school

I was good at sums at school.

story

She read us a story.

very

It was very hot in Seoul today.

361	**application** [æpləkéiʃən]	몡 적용, 응용, 지원	I got a call that my application was lost. 내 지원서가 분실 되었다고 연락이 왔다.
362	**chair** [tʃɛər]	몡 의자, 의장직	He was rooted to her chair. 그는 의자에 붙박이 듯 앉아 있었다.
363	**document** [dákjumənt]	몡 서류, 문서	There is no signature on this document. 이 서류에는 서명이 없습니다.
364	**food** [fuːd]	몡 음식, 식품	Save me some food. 내 음식좀 남겨줘.
365	**impossible** [impásəbl]	혱 불가능한, 난감함	Turn the impossible into possible. 불가능을 가능으로 바꿔라.
366	**method** [méθəd]	몡 방법	The method is not a good choice. 그 방법은 좋은 선택이 아니다.
367	**pattern** [pǽtərn]	몡 (정형화된) 양식	That pattern is so hard to come by. 그런 모양은 구하기가 힘들다.
368	**science** [sáiəns]	몡 과학	She failed his science class. 그녀는 과학수업에서 낙제했다.
369	**straight** [streit]	閉 곧장, 곧바로, 똑바로 혱 일자로	Throw the ball straight! 공을 똑바로 던져라!
370	**view** [vjuː]	몡 견해, 관점, 전망	This room has a beautiful view. 이 방은 전망이 아주 좋다.

● 단어와 문장을 따라 쓰세요.

application
I got a call that my application was lost.

chair
He was rooted to her chair.

document
There is no signature on this document.

food
Save me some food.

impossible
Turn the impossible into possible.

method
The method is not a good choice.

pattern
That pattern is so hard to come by.

science
She failed his science class.

straight
Throw the ball straight!

view
This room has a beautiful view.

371	**area** [ɛ́əriə]	명 지역, 구역	They live in a very select area. 그들은 고급 지역에 산다.
372	**chance** [tʃæns]	명 기회, 가능성	Chance is fair to anyone. 기회는 누구에게나 공평하다.
373	**does** [dəz]	통 do의 3인칭 단수 현재형	She does look tired. 그녀는 무척 피곤해 보인다.
374	**foot** [fut]	명 발, 발 부분	He was standing on one foot. 그는 한 발로 서 있었다.
375	**inch** [intʃ]	명 조금, 약간, 인치	A 32-inch monitor on the desktop! 32인치 모티터에 데스트 탑.
376	**middle** [mídl]	명 중앙, 가운데, 중간	He was standing in the middle of the road. 그는 도로 한 가운데 서 있었다.
377	**pay** [pei]	통 지불하다 명 급여	I will pay the salary next week. 월급은 다음주에 지불하겠습니다.
378	**score** [skɔːr]	명 득점, 스코어	What's the score for the game? 그 경기 점수가 어떻게 되죠?
379	**strange** [streindʒ]	형 이상한 낯선	I feel very strange. 기분이 매우 이상하다.
380	**village** [vílidʒ]	명 마을, 부락	About 50 people live in this village. 이 마을에는 50 여명이 살고 있다.

area
They live in a very select area.

chance
Chance is fair to anyone.

does
She does look tired.

foot
He was standing on one foot.

inch
A 32-inch monitor on the desktop!

middle
He was standing in the middle of the road.

pay
I will pay the salary next week.

score
What's the score for the game?

strange
I feel very strange.

village
About 50 people live in this village.

381	**arm** [aːrm]	몡 팔, 소매	My arm still hurts. 아직도 팔이 아프다.
382	**change** [tʃeindʒ]	통 변화시키다, 바꾸다 몡 변화	I want to change my doctor. 나의 담당 의사 선생님을 바꾸고 싶다.
383	**dollar** [dálər]	몡 달러	The US dollar can be used anywhere in the world. 미국 달러는 세계 어디에서나 사용할 수 있다.
384	**for** [fər]	젠 (…을 돕기) 위해 젠 …에 대해	Can you order a book for me? 나를 위해 책을 주문해 줄수 있겠습니까?
385	**include** [inklúːd]	통 포함하다, ~ 포함 시키다.	The rate does not include delivery. 그 가격에는 배달료가 들어가 있지 않다.
386	**might** [mait]	조, 통 ~할지도 모르다	She might be useful to us. 그녀는 우리에게 도움이 될지도 모른다.
387	**payment** [péimənt]	몡 지불, 지급	What are the terms of payment? 지급 조건은 어떻게 되나요?
388	**sea** [siː]	몡 바다	A hotel room with sea view. 바다가 보이는 호텔 객실
389	**stream** [striːm]	몡 개울, 시내	I saw a frog in a stream. 개울에서 개구리를 본 적 있다.
390	**visit** [vízit]	통 방문하다, 찾아가다.	I need to visit my home country. 고국에 다녀 와야 겠어요.

● 단어와 문장을 따라 쓰세요.

arm
My arm still hurts.

change
I want to change my doctor.

dollar
The US dollar can be used anywhere in the world.

for
Can you order a book for me?

include
The rate does not include delivery.

might
She might be useful to us.

payment
What are the terms of payment?

sea
A hotel room with sea view.

stream
I saw a frog in a stream.

visit
I need to visit my home country.

391	**army** [áːrmi]	몡 군대, 부대	I decided to join the army. 나는 군대에 가기로 결심했다.
392	**character** [kǽriktər]	몡 성격, 기질	She's a larger than life character. 그녀는 허풍을 떠는 성격이다.
393	**don't** [dount]	do not의 축약형	Don't say things you don't mean. 마음에도 없는 말 하지 마세요.
394	**force** [fɔːrs]	몡 물리력, 힘 통 ~강요하다.	The moon exerts a force on the earth. 달은 지구에 힘을 가합니다.
395	**independent** [indipéndənt]	혱 독립된, 독립적인	She is strong and independent. 그녀는 강하고 독립적이다.
396	**mile** [mail]	몡 마일(거리단위)	The beach is a mile away. 해변을 1마일 떨어져 있다.
397	**people** [píːpl]	몡 사람들	Many people need your love. 많은 사람들이 너의 사랑을 필요로 하고 있다.
398	**search** [səːrtʃ]	몡 찾기, 수색	The search was canceled because of the rain. 비 때문에 수색 작업이 취소 되었다.
399	**street** [striːt]	몡 거리, 도로	He's sweeping the street. 그는 거리를 청소하고 있다.
400	**voice** [vɔis]	몡 목소리, 음성	She has a high voice. 그녀는 목소리는 고음이다.

army
I decided to join the army.

character
She's a larger than life character.

don't
Don't say things you don't mean.

force
The moon exerts a force on the earth.

independent
She is strong and independent.

mile
The beach is a mile away.

people
Many people need your love.

search
The search was canceled because of the rain.

street
He's sweeping the street.

voice
She has a high voice.

A 주어진 문장에 맞는 단어를 보기에서 찾아 문장을 완성하세요.

❶ A Tiger is a dangerous _____ . 동물

❷ I _____ some fish by fishing. 잡다

❸ Your _____ is exactly right. 대답, 답

❹ What was the _____ of the fire? 원인, 이유

❺ I didn't eat _____ meat. 전혀, 조금도

❻ He was a _____ salesman. 휴대폰

❼ Is _____ there? 아무도, 아무라도

❽ We wanted a town youth _____ . 종합시설, 센터

❾ When will the stars _____ ? 나타나다, 보이다

❿ The house was built in the 16th _____ . 100년, 1세기

> **appear anybody any answer animal caught century center cell-phone cause**

B 해석을 보고 빈칸에 해당되는 단어를 보기에서 찾아 적으세요.

❶ _____ the sick from the others 환자를 격리하다.

　 _____ one's hair in the middle 가르마를 가운데 타다.

❷ a window _____ 진열장의 상품 진열

　 _____ bravery 용기를 보이다

❸ ceramic _____ tiles 세라믹 바닥 타일

❹ _____ shoes (굽이) 낮은 신발

　 The high notes were slightly _____ . 높은 음들이 약간 낮았다.

❺ the _____ sound of music 멀리서 들려오는 음악 소리

　 _____ stars/planets 먼 곳에 있는 별들/행성들

❻ to _____ the Atlantic 대서양을 위를 날다

　 to _____ at the speed of sound 음속의 속도로 비행하다

❼ a garden full of _____ 꽃이 가득한 정원

　 the _____ of one's youth 한창 젊을 때

> **flower   fly   display   distant   divide   flat   floor**

C 보기에 주어진 단어의 설명입니다. 해당되는 단어를 찾아 적으세요.

❶ 라는 뜻[의미]이다, …을 뜻하다[의미하다] _____

❷ 다치게[아프게] 하다 _____

❸ 특정 상황에서 해야 할 일에 대한 발상 _____

❹ (우연히) 만나다 _____

❺ 서두르다, 급히 하다 (유의어 rush) _____

❻ (한 음악 작품의 주된 가락을 이루는) 선율 _____

❼ (식용하는 짐승·조류의) 고기 _____

> idea   hurt   melody   hurry   meat   mean   meet

D 주어진 해석에 맞는 영어단어로 퍼즐을 완성하세요.

Across

4. 나눗셈, 나누기
7. 일부, 부분
8. 누구든지, 아무나
9. 바닥

Down

1. 나누다, 나뉘다
2. 전시, 진열
3. 대답, 회신
5. 돌, 돌맹이
6. 꽃

A 주어진 문장에 맞는 단어를 보기에서 찾아 문장을 완성하세요.

1. He peeled and quartered an _____. 사과
2. He looks _____ to win an Oscar. 확신, 틀림없는
3. I got a call that my _____ was lost. 지원서, 신청서
4. He was rooted to her _____. 의자
5. They live in a very select _____. 지역, 구역
6. _____ is fair to anyone. 기회
7. My _____ still hurts. 팔
8. I want to _____ my doctor. 바꾸다, 변하다
9. I decided to join the _____. 군대, 육군
10. She's a larger than life _____. 성격, 특징, 캐릭터

certain character change chair chance certain army area arm apple

B 해석을 보고 빈칸에 해당되는 단어를 보기에서 찾아 적으세요.

1. to _____ a diet/recipe 다이어트/조리법을 따라 하다

   _____ a person in[out] …을 따라 들어가다[나가다]
2. Does the price _____ tax? 그 가격에 세금이 포함되어 있나요?
3. Save the _____ before closing. 창을 닫기 전에 문서를 저장하라.

   an official[a public] _____ 공문서
4. We came on _____. 우리는 걸어 왔다.

   with heavy _____ 무거운 걸음걸이로
5. a peace-keeping _____ 평화 유지군

   magnetic / centrifugal _____ 자력/원심력
6. see[consult] the _____ 의사의 진찰을 받다, 병원에 가다

   a car _____ 자동차 정비공
7. a shortage of _____ 식량 부족

   He's off his _____. 그는 식음을 전폐했다.

force follow foot food include doctor document

C 보기에 주어진 단어의 설명입니다. 해당되는 단어를 찾아 적으세요.

❶ ~을 (~에) 포함시키다 (반의어 exclude) _____

❷ 상상하다, (마음속으로) 그리다 _____

❸ 국가가 독립된 (유의어 self-governing) _____

❹ 불가능한 (반의어 possible) _____

❺ 중앙, (한)가운데, 중간 _____

❻ (가능성을 나타내어) …일지도 모른다 _____

❼ 마일, 거리 단위. 1609미터 _____

> **may   independent   include   middle   impossible   mile   imagine**

D 주어진 해석에 맞는 영어단어로 퍼즐을 완성하세요.

Across

3. 마을
4. 상상하다, 그리다
5. 이상한, 낯선
7. 변화시키다, 바꾸다
8. 중앙, 가운데

Down

1. 지불, 지급
2. 과학
5. 학교
6. 의자

401	**arrange** [əréindʒ]	동 마련하다, 정리하다, 배열하다	Can we arrange a meeting soon? 회의를 빨리 잡을 수 있을까요?
402	**charge** [tʃaːrdʒ]	명 요금 동 청구하다.	Breakfast is added without extra charge. 아침식사는 요금 추가 없이 제공 된다.
403	**done** [dʌn]	형 다 된, 완료된 형 완전히 요리된, 푹 삶은, 바싹 구운	The meat isn't quite done yet. 고기가 아직 덜 익었다.
404	**forest** [fɔːrɪst]	명 숲, 삼림	We walked through the forest. 우리는 숲속을 걸어 지나갔다.
405	**indicate** [índikèit]	동 나타나다, 내비치다.	The signs indicate prices. 표지판은 가격을 보여준다.
406	**milk** [milk]	명 우유	You must drink one glass of milk a day. 우유는 하루에 한잔 꼭 마셔야 한다.
407	**perfect** [pə́ːrfikt]	형 완벽한	It was a perfect game. 완벽한 경기였다.
408	**season** [síːzn]	명 계절, 시즌	It's a shame the baseball season is over. 야구 시즌이 끝나 아쉽다.
409	**stretch** [stretʃ]	동 늘어나다, 신축성이 있다	Stretch and then sleep. 쭉 뻗은 다음 주무세요.
410	**wait** [weit]	동 기다리다.	Could you wait a moment, please? 잠깐만 기다려 주시겠습니까?

단어와 문장을 따라 쓰세요.

arrange
Can we arrange a meeting soon?

charge
Breakfast is added without extra charge.

done
The meat isn't quite done yet.

forest
We walked through the forest.

indicate
The signs indicate prices.

milk
You must drink one glass of milk a day.

perfect
It was a perfect game.

season
It's a shame the baseball season is over.

stretch
Stretch and then sleep.

wait
Could you wait a moment, please?

411	**arrive** [əráiv]	동 배달되다, 도착하다	I have to arrive by 2 at the latest. 나는 늦어도 2시까지 도착해야 한다.
412	**chart** [tʃaːrt]	명 도표, 차트	He was the number one player on the chart. 그는 차트에서 1위를 차지했다.
413	**double** ['dʌbl]	명 두 배, 갑절	A fight broke out over double parking. 이중 주차 문제로 싸움이 일어났다.
414	**form** [fɔːrm]	명 종류, 유형 동 형성되다, 형성시키다	Drivers must sign a form. 운전자들은 양식에 서명해야 한다.
415	**industry** [índəstri]	명 산업, 공업, 제조업	He got a job in industry. 그는 제조업 분야에 일자리를 잡았다.
416	**million** [míljən]	수 100만	I need two million won right now. 나는 당장 2백만원이 필요하다.
417	**perhaps** [pərhǽps]	부 아마, 어쩌면	Perhaps it is a vegetarian cat. 아마 채식주의 고양이인가 보다.
418	**seat** [siːt]	명 자리, 좌석	The safety belt must be worn. 안전 벨트는 꼭 착용해야 한다.
419	**strong** [strɔːŋ]	형 튼튼한, 강한, 힘센	He wasn't a strong swimmer. 그는 강한 수영 선수가 아니었다.
420	**walk** [wɔːk]	동 걷다, 걸어가다 명 산책	I walk to work most mornings. 나는 대부분 아침에 걸어서 출근한다.

arrive

I have to arrive by 2 at the latest.

chart

He was the number one player on the chart.

double

A fight broke out over double parking.

form

Drivers must sign a form.

industry

He got a job in industry.

million

I need two million won right now.

perhaps

Perhaps it is a vegetarian cat.

seat

The safety belt must be worn.

strong

He wasn't a strong swimmer.

walk

I walk to work most mornings.

421	**art** [a:rt]	몡 미술, 미술품, 예술	His picture is hung in the Museum of Art. 그의 그림이 미술관에 전시되어 있다.
422	**check** [tʃek]	통 살피다. 확인하다. 몡 확인, 점검	Do you know your check-in time? 탑승 수속시간을 알고 있나요?
423	**down** [daun]	閉 낮은 쪽으로, 아래로, 내려 놓다.	Put it down over there. 이것을 저기에 내려 놓다.
424	**forward** [fɔ́:rwərd]	閉 앞으로	She took two steps forward. 그녀가 앞으로 두 걸음 뗐다.
425	**insect** [ínsekt]	몡 곤충	A small insect flies around the room. 작은 곤충 한마리가 방에 날아 다닌다.
426	**mind** [maind]	통 상관하다, 개의하다 몡 마음, 정신	She has a closed mind. 그녀는 마음이 닫혀있다.
427	**period** ['pɪr-]	몡 기간, 시기	I get sensitive during the exam period. 시험기간에는 예민해 진다.
428	**second** [sékənd]	혱 두번째. 제2의	Could you tell us about your second album? 두번째 앨범에 대해 설명해 주시겠어요?
429	**student** [stju:dnt]	몡 학생	Do you have a student discount? 학생 할인이 되나요?
430	**wall** [wɔ:l]	몡 담, 벽	The boys climbed over the wall. 그 남자 애들이 담을 넘어갔다.

단어와 문장을 따라 쓰세요.

art

His picture is hung in the Museum of Art.

check

Do you know your check-in time?

down

Put it down over there.

forward

She took two steps forward.

insect

A small insect flies around the room.

mind

She has a closed mind.

period

I get sensitive during the exam period.

second

Could you tell us about your second album?

student

Do you have a student discount?

wall

The boys climbed over the wall.

431	**as** [əz]	전 …처럼,~같이 전 (자격·기능 등이) …로(서) 부 …만큼 …한	Can you run as fast as Minho? 너는 민호처럼 빨리 달리수 있니?
432	**cheese** [tʃiːz]	명 치즈	Breakfast is bread and cheese. 아침은 빵과 치즈이다.
433	**dramatic** [drəˈmætɪk]	형 감격적인, 인상적인, 극적인	Her life is dramatic. 그녀의 삶은 극적이다.
434	**found** [faund]	동 설립하다. 세우다. 타 만들다, 근거를 두다	The accused was found innocent. 그 피해자는 무죄로 밝혀졌다.
435	**instant** [ínstənt]	형 즉각적인, 인스턴트의	The store is full of instant food. 상점에 즉석요리가 넘쳐난다.
436	**mine** [main]	대 나의 것 명 광산	Your shoes are the same brand as mine. 너의 신발은 나의 신발과 같은 브랜드이다.
437	**person** [pə́ːrsn]	명 사람, 개인	I am a very outgoing person. 나는 매우 외향적인 사람이다.
438	**section** [sékʃən]	명 부분, 부문, 구획	Keeping an eye on the section? 그 구역을 관심있게 보나요?
439	**study** [stʌdi]	명 학업, 학문 동 공부하다.	I'm trying to study. 나 지금 공부하려고 해.
440	**want** [want]	동 원하다, 바라다, …하고 싶어하다 명 원하는것, 필요한 것	I want the job. 나는 직업을 갖고 싶어.

as

Can you run as fast as Minho?

cheese

Breakfast is bread and cheese.

dramatic

Her life is dramatic.

found

The accused was found innocent.

instant

The store is full of instant food.

mine

Your shoes are the same brand as mine.

person

I am a very outgoing person.

section

Keeping an eye on the section?

study

I'm trying to study.

want

I want the job.

441	**aside** [əsáid]	男 한쪽으로, 따로	She laid aside his book and stood up. 그녀가 책을 한쪽으로 밀쳐놓고 일어났다.
442	**chick** [tʃik]	名 병아리, 새끼 새	He was selling a small chick in front of the school. 그는 학교 앞에서 작은 병아리를 팔고 있었다.
443	**draw** [drɔ:]	動 그리다, 끌어당기다.	The children love to draw and color. 아이들은 그림을 그리고 색칠하는 것을 좋아한다.
444	**fraction** ['frækʃn]	名 부분, 일부	at a mere fraction of the cost. 그 비용의 겨우 일부분
445	**insurance** [inʃúərəns]	名 보험, 보험료	Cancer insurance is essential. 암 보험은 꼭 필요하다.
446	**minister** [mínəstər]	名 성직자, 장관(총리), 목사	He is the new prime minister of the United Kingdom. 그는 영국에 새로운 총리이다.
447	**pick** [pik]	動 고르다, 선택하다, 뽑다	Can you pick me up at 9 am? 아침 9시에 저를 태우러 올 수 있나요?
448	**see** [si:]	動 보다, 목격하다. 他 참조하다	How lovely to see you! 너를 만나서 정말 기뻐!
449	**subject** [sʌbdʒikt]	名 학과, 과목	Biology is my favorite subject. 생물학은 내가 좋아하는 과목이다.
450	**war** [wɔ:r]	名 전쟁	Many lives were destroyed in the war. 그 전쟁에서 많은 사람이 죽었다.

단어와 문장을 따라 쓰세요.

aside
She laid aside his book and stood up.

chick
He was selling a small chick in front of the school.

draw
The children love to draw and color.

fraction
at a mere fraction of the cost

insurance
Cancer insurance is essential.

minister
He is the new prime minister of the United Kingdom.

pick
Can you pick me up at 9 am?

see
How lovely to see you!

subject
Biology is my favorite subject.

war
Many lives were destroyed in the war.

451	**ask** [æsk]	통 묻다, 물어 보다 통 부탁하다, 요청하다.	Can I ask a question? 질문하나 해도 될까요?
452	**child** [ʧaild]	명 아이, 어린이	I lived in Paris when I was a child. 나는 어렸을때 파리에 살았다.
453	**dream** [driːm]	명 꿈	I went to Everland last night in my dream. 어제밤 꿈에 에버랜드에 놀러 갔다.
454	**free** [friː]	형 자유, 자유롭다	All the tickets to the games are free. 경기의 모든 표는 공짜이다.
455	**interest** [íntərəst]	명 관심, 흥미, 호기심	His main interest is cars. 그의 주 관심사는 차이다.
456	**minute** [mínit]	명 (시간의) 분 형 극미한, 극히 작은	It's only a five-minute taxi ride away. 그곳은 택시로 5분 거리에 있다.
457	**picture** [píkʧər]	명 그림, 사진. 통 …를 상상하다	They're drawing a picture. 그들이 그림을 그리고 있다.
458	**seed** [siːd]	명 씨, 씨앗, 종자	The seed has become a good plant. 그 씨앗은 좋은 식물이 되었다.
459	**substance** ['sʌbstəns]	명 본질, 핵심, 요지	This is a very dangerous substance. 이것은 매우 위험한 물질이다.
460	**warm** [wɔːrm]	형 따뜻한, 따스한, 훈훈한	This sleeping bag is very warm. 이 침낭은 매우 따뜻하다.

ask
Can I ask a question?

child
I lived in Paris when I was a child.

dream
I went to Everland last night in my dream.

free
All the tickets to the games are free.

interest
His main interest is cars.

minute
It's only a five-minute taxi ride away.

picture
They're drawing a picture.

seed
The seed has become a good plant.

substance
This is a very dangerous substance.

warm
This sleeping bag is very warm.

461	**at** [ət]	전 <장소> …에 전 <시간> …에	I was good at sums at school. 나는 학교에 다닐때 수학을 잘했다.
462	**childhood** [ʧáildhùd]	명 어린시절	I remember a pleasant childhood. 즐거운 어린시절이 기억난다.
463	**dress** [dres]	명 드레스, 원피스	Your dress is so beautiful. 너의 드레스가 너무 아름답다.
464	**freedom** [frí:dəm]	명 자유	I cried for freedom. 자유를 달라고 외쳤다.
465	**invent** [invént]	동 발명하다, 지어내다.	I want to invent special glasses. 나는 특별한 안경을 발명하고 싶다.
466	**miss** [mis]	동 놓치다, 지나치다	I never miss going there. 나는 그곳에 가는 것을 빼먹은 적이 없다.
467	**piece** [pi:s]	명 조각, 부분	a piece of meat. 고기 한 조각
468	**seem** [si:m]	동 ~ 보이다. ~ 인 것 같다.	You seem nervous. 너는 긴장한 것처럼 보인다.
469	**success** [səksés]	명 성공, 성과	She was overjoyed at my success. 그녀는 나의 성공을 기뻐했다.
470	**was** [wəz]	동 있다. 있었다, 존재하다	He was born poor. 그는 가난한 집에서 태어났습니다.

● 단어와 문장을 따라 쓰세요.

at

I was good at sums at school.

childhood

I remember a pleasant childhood.

dress

Your dress is so beautiful.

freedom

I cried for freedom.

invent

I want to invent special glasses.

miss

I never miss going there.

piece

a piece of meat.

seem

You seem nervous.

success

She was overjoyed at my success.

was

He was born poor.

471	**atom** [ǽtəm]	몡 원자	An atom is the smallest unit of matter. 원자는 물질의 제일 작은 단위이다.
472	**children** [tʃíldrən]	몡 Child의 복수, 아이들	My children are my life. 내 아이들은 내 목숨과 같다.
473	**drink** [driŋk]	몡 음료, 마실 것, 술	I want to drink a cool drink because I'm thirsty. 나는 갈증이 나서 시원한 음료를 마시고 싶다.
474	**fresh** [freʃ]	혱 신선한, 생생한	I want fresh milk now. 나는 지금 신선한 우유를 마시고 싶다.
475	**iron** [áiərn]	몡 다리미, Fe(철)	He had a will of iron. 그는 의지가 강철 같았다.
476	**mistake** [mistéik]	몡 실수, 잘못	He admitted to making a mistake. 그는 실수를 인정했다.
477	**place** [pleis]	몡 장소, 곳 통 놓다, 설치하다.	This is a good place for lunch. 이곳은 점심먹기에 좋은 장소이다.
478	**select** [silékt]	통 선발, 선택하다	Please select between the two. 둘 중 하나를 선택하세요.
479	**such** [sətʃ]	혬, 떼 앞에, 이미 언급한, 그러한 혬, 떼 그정도의	Don't be such a fool! 바보같이 굴지 마!
480	**wash** [waʃ]	통 씻다	It's so hard today that it's hard to wash. 오늘은 너무 힘들어서 씻기도 힘들다.

atom
An atom is the smallest unit of matter.

children
My children are my life.

drink
I want to drink a cool drink because I'm thirsty.

fresh
I want fresh milk now.

iron
He had a will of iron.

mistake
He admitted to making a mistake.

place
This is a good place for lunch.

select
Please select between the two.

such
Don't be such a fool!

wash
It's so hard today that it's hard to wash.

481	**average** [ˈævərɪdʒ]	형 보통의, 일반적인	We eat out four times a month on average. 우리는 한달에 평균 4번정도 외식을 한다.
482	**choose** [tʃuːz]	통 선택하다, 선정하다.	You choose, I'm not a choice. 네가 선택해, 나는 선택하기 힘드네.
483	**drive** [draiv]	통 (차량을) 몰다, 운전하다	Don't drink and drive. 음주 운전 하지 마세요.
484	**friend** [frend]	명 친구	This is my friend Minho. 나의 친구 민호입니다.
485	**island** [áilənd]	명 섬	The island country is slowly sinking. 이 섬나라는 점점 가라앉고 있습니다.
486	**mix** [miks]	통 섞이다, 혼합하다.	Water and oil do not mix. 물과 기름은 섞이지 않는다.
487	**plain** [plein]	형 숨김없는, 솔직한, 있는 그대로의	My question to you is plain. 너에 대한 나의 질문은 평범해.
488	**self** [self]	명 모습, 본모습	This is my true self. 이것의 나의 본모습입니다.
489	**sudden** [sʌdn]	형 갑작스러운, 급작스러운	The weather got cold all of a sudden! 날씨가 갑자기 추워졌어!
490	**watch** [watʃ]	통 보다, 지켜보다, 주시하다	My watch is five minutes slow. 내 시계는 5분 늦다.

단어와 문장을 따라 쓰세요.

average

We eat out four times a month on average.

choose

You choose, I'm not a choice.

drive

Don't drink and drive.

friend

This is my friend Minho.

island

The island country is slowly sinking.

mix

Water and oil do not mix.

plain

My question to you is plain.

self

This is my true self.

sudden

The weather got cold all of a sudden!

watch

My watch is five minutes slow.

491	**baby** [béibi]	명 아기	The baby peed. 아기가 오줌을 쌌다.
492	**circle** [sə́:rkl]	명 동그라미, 원	They sat in a circle. 그들은 동그랗게 앉았다.
493	**drop** [drap]	동 떨어지다.	Drop the gun! 총을 내려 놔!
494	**from** [frəm]	전 …에서(부터) 전 (시작, 시각) …부터	Where are you from? 어디에서 오셨나요?
495	**job** [dʒab]	명 일, 직장, 일자리	I have a desk job. 나는 사무직에 종사한다.
496	**modern** [mádərn]	형 현대적인, 모던한	Simple modern design is in vogue these days. 요즘은 단순한 현대 디자인이 유행하고 있다.
497	**plan** [plæn]	명 계획 동 계획하다	He was interested in my plan. 그는 내 계획에 관심이 있었다.
498	**sell** [sel]	동 팔다.	Department stores sell many kinds of goods. 백화점은 많은 종류의 상품을 판다.
499	**sugar** [ʃúgər]	명 설탕	Don't put too much sugar in your food. 음식에 설탕을 너무 많이 넣지 마세요.
500	**water** [wɔ́:tər]	명 물 동 물을주다	She fell into the water. 그녀가 물속으로 떨어졌다.

baby
The baby peed.

circle
They sat in a circle.

drop
Drop the gun!

from
Where are you from?

job
I have a desk job.

modern
Simple modern design is in vogue these days.

plan
He was interested in my plan.

sell
Department stores sell many kinds of goods.

sugar
Don't put too much sugar in your food.

water
She fell into the water.

A 주어진 문장에 맞는 단어를 보기에서 찾아 문장을 완성하세요.

❶ Can we _____ a meeting soon? 마련하다, 주선하다

❷ Breakfast is added without extra _____. 요금

❸ I have to _____ by 2 at the latest. 도착하다

❹ He was the number one player on the _____. 도표, 차트

❺ His picture is hung in the Museum of _____. 미술품

❻ Do you know your _____ time? 숙박절차, 체크인

❼ Can you run as fast _____ Minho? ~처럼

❽ Breakfast is bread and _____. 치즈

❾ She laid _____ his book and stood up. 따로, 한쪽으로

❿ He was selling a small _____ in front of the school. 병아리

| chick cheese check aside as charge art arrive chart arrange |

B 해석을 보고 빈칸에 해당되는 단어를 보기에서 찾아 적으세요.

❶ to _____ a picture/diagram/graph 그림/도표/그래프를 그리다

The train _____ in. 기차가 들어왔다.

❷ from this day _____ 이 날 이후 앞으로

the _____ cabins 앞쪽 객실들

❸ an application/entry/order _____ 지원서/참가 신청서/주문서

to fill out a _____ 서식을 작성하다

❹ in a _____ of a second 순식간에

a _____ of the crowd 군중의 일부

❺ a tropical _____ 열대 숲

a _____ fire 산불

❻ _____ doors 이중문

a _____ bed/room 2인용 침대/2인실

❼ Please sit _____. 앉으세요.

Turn the music _____! 음악 좀 낮춰!

| draw forest fraction form forward double down |

124

C 보기에 주어진 단어의 설명입니다. 해당되는 단어를 찾아 적으세요.

❶ (사실임·존재함을) 나타내다 _____

❷ 100만 _____

❸ 마음, 정신 _____

❹ 산업, 공업, 제조업 _____

❺ 즉각적인 (유의어 immediate) _____

❻ 보험 (참조 National Insurance) _____

❼ (영국을 비롯한 많은 국가들에서) 장관, 각료 _____

> instant   minister   million   insurance   mind   industry   indicate

D 주어진 해석에 맞는 영어단어로 퍼즐을 완성하세요.

Across

2. 계절
4. 앞으로
7. 성직자, 장관
9. 튼튼한, 강한

Down

1. 부분, 구획
3. 완벽한
5. 숲, 살림
6. 두번째
8. 사람, 개인

A 주어진 문장에 맞는 단어를 보기에서 찾아 문장을 완성하세요.

❶ Can I _____ a question? 묻다, 물어보다

❷ I lived in Paris when I was a _____. 아이, 어린이

❸ I was good at sums _____ school. ~에서, ~에

❹ I remember a pleasant _____. 어린 시절

❺ An _____ is the smallest unit of matter. 원자

❻ My _____ are my life. 아이들

❼ We eat out four times a month on _____. 평균, 보통

❽ You _____, I'm not a choice. 택하다, 고르다

❾ The _____ peed. 아기

❿ They sat in a _____. 원형, 동그라미

child   atom   circle   childhood   children   average   baby   ask   choose   at

B 해석을 보고 빈칸에 해당되는 단어를 보기에서 찾아 적으세요.

❶ I feel ready to _____. 나는 금방이라도 쓰러질 것 같아

not a _____ of kindness 친절이라고는 조금도 없는

❷ a _____ of water 물 한 잔

food and _____ 음식물

❸ Admission is _____. 입장료는 무료이다.

virtually fat-_____ yogurt 지방이 거의 없는 요구르트

❹ _____ of speech/thought/expression/worship 표현/사상/표현/종교의 자유

_____ of action/choice 행동/선택의 자유

❺ a display of _____ cars 멋진 차의 전시

awake from a _____ 꿈에서 깨다

❻ Is this milk _____? 이 우유는 신선한가요?

_____ tracks in the snow 눈 위에 새로 난 발자국

❼ a long white _____ 흰색의 긴 드레스[원피스]

He has no _____ sense. 그는 옷에 대한 감각이 없다.

freedom   dream   dress   fresh   drop   free   drink

C 보기에 주어진 단어의 설명입니다. 해당되는 단어를 찾아 적으세요.

① 현대의, 근대의 (유의어 contemporary) _____

② Fe 철, 쇠; 철분 _____

③ 발명하다, (사실이 아닌 것을) 지어내다 _____

④ 실수, 잘못 _____

⑤ ~ A and B (together) 섞이다, 혼합[배합]되다 _____

⑥ (정기적으로 보수를 받고 하는) 일, 직장, 일자리 _____

⑦ (치거나 잡거나 닿지 못하고) 놓치다 _____

> **invent**　　**mix**　　**job**　　**iron**　　**miss**　　**mistake**　　**modern**

D 주어진 해석에 맞는 영어단어로 퍼즐을 완성하세요.

Across

3. 동그라미, 원
7. 그림, 사진
8. 운전하다
9. 보통의, 일반적인
10. 신선한, 생생한

Down

1. 꿈
2. 실수, 잘못
4. 조각, 부분
5. 성공, 성과
6. 갑작스러운

501	**back** [bæk]	형 뒤쪽의 명 등, (등)허리	He'll be back on Monday. 그는 월요일에 돌아올 것이다.
502	**city** [síti]	명 도시, 시	He lives to the west of the city. 그는 그 시의 서쪽에 산다.
503	**dry** [drai]	형 마른, 건조한	The dry weather will continue. 건조한 날이 계속 되겠다.
504	**front** [frʌnt]	명 앞면, 앞쪽	He's got a front tooth missing. 그는 앞니 한 개가 없다.
505	**join** [dʒɔin]	동 연결하다, 합쳐지다	Would you like to join us for dinner? 우리와 함께 저녁 식사 할래요?
506	**moment** [móumənt]	명 잠깐, 잠시	Please keep my bag for a moment. 잠시 제 가방을 보관해 주세요.
507	**plane** [plein]	명 비행기 형 평평한	The plane landed in Seoul. 그 비행기는 서울에 도착했다.
508	**send** [send]	동 보내다, 발송하다.	Send the urgent items to the air package. 급한 물건은 항공 소포로 보내라.
509	**suggest** [səgdʒést]	동 제안하다, 추천하다.	I'll suggest going by car. 나는 차로 가는 것을 제안할게.
510	**wave** [weiv]	명 파도, 물결	A cold wave hit Europe this winter. 이번 한파가 유럽을 강타했다.

back

He'll be back on Monday.

city

He lives to the west of the city.

dry

The dry weather will continue.

front

He's got a front tooth missing.

join

Would you like to join us for dinner?

moment

Please keep my bag for a moment.

plane

The plane landed in Seoul.

send

Send the urgent items to the air package.

suggest

I'll suggest going by car.

wave

A cold wave hit Europe this winter.

511	**bad** [bæd]	형 안 좋은, 불쾌한, 나쁜	No one is bad from birth. 태어날때부터 나쁜 사람은 없다
512	**claim** [kleim]	통 주장하다, 요청하다.	The goods exported were made a claim. 수출품에 클레임이 제기 되었다.
513	**duck** [dʌk]	명 오리	Duck meat is not sold here. 이곳에서는 오리 고기를 팔지 않는다.
514	**fruit** [fru:t]	명 과일	The fruit is being harvested. 과일을 수확하고 있다.
515	**journalist** [dʒə́:rnəlist]	명 저널리스트, 기자	She is an excellent journalist. 그녀는 유능한 기자이다.
516	**money** [mʌni]	명 돈, 금전, 재산	Money is round, and rolls away. 돈은 둥글다, 그래서 굴러다닌다.
517	**planet** [plǽnit]	명 행성	The planet is only seen by a telescope. 그 행성은 망원경으로만 보인다.
518	**sense** [sens]	통 감지하다, 느끼다. 명 감각	He has a poor sense of fashion. 그는 패션 감각이 좋지 않다.
519	**suit** [su:t]	명 정장	I wore a black suit to attend the funeral. 장례식에 참석하기 위해 검은색 정장을 입었다.
520	**way** [wei]	명 방식, 태도, 방법 부 아주멀리	Which way did they go? 그들이 어느 쪽으로 갔나요?

bad

No one is bad from birth.

claim

The goods exported were made a claim.

duck

Duck meat is not sold here.

fruit

The fruit is being harvested.

journalist

She is an excellent journalist.

money

Money is round, and rolls away.

planet

The planet is only seen by a telescope.

sense

He has a poor sense of fashion.

suit

I wore a black suit to attend the funeral.

way

Which way did they go?

521	**balance** [bǽləns]	몡 균형	Yoga is important to balance your body. 요가는 몸의 균형을 잡는게 중요하다.
522	**class** [klæs]	몡 학급, 수업	She works hard in class. 그녀는 수업시간에 열심히 공부한다.
523	**during** [djúəriŋ]	젠 ~하는 동안, ~ 하는 중에	I lost something precious during the move. 이사하는 동안 아끼던 물건이 사라졌다.
524	**full** [ful]	혱 ~가득한, ~그득한	I'm full. 나는 배가불러
525	**joy** [dʒɔi]	몡 기쁨 환희	Everybody jumped for joy. 모두 기뻐서 뛰었다.
526	**month** [mʌnθ]	몡 달, 월	It takes over a month. 한 달 넘게 걸린다.
527	**plant** [plænt]	몡 식물, 공장 통 심다.	This plant blooms often. 이 식물은 종종 꽃이 핀다.
528	**sent** [sent]	통 send의 과거, 과거분사	He sometimes sent me a message. 그는 가끔 내게 메시지를 보냈다.
529	**summer** [sʌ́mər]	몡 여름	Do you have any plans for the summer? 여름에 무슨 계획 있으세요?
530	**we** [wi;]	때 ('나'를 포함)우리, 저희	we go to a doctor. 우리는 의사에게 가야한다.

단어와 문장을 따라 쓰세요.

balance
Yoga is important to balance your body.

class
She works hard in class.

during
I lost something precious during the move.

full
I'm full.

joy
Everybody jumped for joy.

month
It takes over a month.

plant
This plant blooms often.

sent
He sometimes sent me a message.

summer
Do you have any plans for the summer?

we
we go to a doctor.

531	**ball** [bɔ:l]	명 공	Who is kicking the ball? 누가 공을 차고 있나요?
532	**classroom** [klǽsrùːm]	명 교실	The classroom is noisy when it's time to rest. 쉬는 시간이 되면 교실은 시끄럽다.
533	**duty** [djúːti]	명 직무, 임무	The duty to the family is the first. 가족에 대한 의무가 첫번째다.
534	**fun** [fʌn]	명 재미, 장난	I had fun at the party yesterday. 어제 파티는 재미있었다.
535	**judgment** [dʒʌdʒmənt]	명 판단, 심사, 판결, 재판	The judgment of man is fallible. 인간의 판단은 틀리기 쉽다.
536	**moon** [muːn]	명 달	The first Apollo moon landing. 최초로 아폴로 달 착륙
537	**play** [plei]	동 놀다, (게임, 경기) 하다 명 놀이, 연극	How long does the play last? 그 경기는 언제까지 계속 하나요?
538	**sentence** [séntəns]	명 문장 명 형벌 동 (형을) 선고하다	I was very impressed by this sentence. 나는 이 문장에 깊은 감명을 받았다.
539	**sun** [sʌn]	명 해, 태양, 햇빛	I get up with the sun. 나는 해가 뜨는 것과 같이 일어난다.
540	**wear** [wɛər]	동 입고있다.	I have to wear glasses when driving. 나는 운전할때 안경을 써야한다.

ball

Who is kicking the ball?

classroom

The classroom is noisy when it's time to rest.

duty

The duty to the family is the first.

fun

I had fun at the party yesterday.

judgment

The judgment of man is fallible.

moon

The first Apollo moon landing.

play

How long does the play last?

sentence

I was very impressed by this sentence.

sun

I get up with the sun.

wear

I have to wear glasses when driving.

541	**band** [bænd]	명 밴드, 악단	The band was not good at playing. 그 밴드는 연주를 잘하지 못했다.
542	**clean** [kli:n]	형 깨끗한, 깔끔한	You have to wash it clean every day. 매일 깨끗이 씻어야 한다.
543	**each** [i:tʃ]	대 각각, 각자의	We each have our own car. 우리는 각자 자기 차를 가지고 있다.
544	**game** [geim]	명 경기, 시합, 게임	The game ends in a 2-2 tie. 그 게임은 2-2 무승부로 끝났다.
545	**jump** [dʒʌmp]	동 뛰다, 점프하다.	I want to jump high in the sky. 하늘 높이 점프하고 싶다.
546	**more** [mɔ:r]	한 대명사 더 많은 수	I won't say more. 나는 더 이상 말하지 않겠어.
547	**please** [pli:z]	감 부디, 제발, 정말	Please, let me pass the test. 제발 시험에 합격하게 해주세요.
548	**separate** [sépərèit]	형 서로 다른, 별개의, 관련 없는	There are two separate issues here. 여기 두 가지의 개별적인 문제가 있다.
549	**supply** [səplái]	명 공급	The electricity supply here is quite erratic. 이곳은 전기 공급이 상당히 불규칙하다.
550	**weather** [wéðər]	명 날씨, 기상, 일기	I don't like cold weather. 나는 추운 날씨가 싫다.

단어와 문장을 따라 쓰세요.

band

The band was not good at playing.

clean

You have to wash it clean every day.

each

We each have our own car.

game

The game ends in a 2-2 tie.

jump

I want to jump high in the sky.

more

I won't say more.

please

Please, let me pass the test.

separate

There are two separate issues here.

supply

The electricity supply here is quite erratic.

weather

I don't like cold weather.

551	**bank** [bæŋk]	명 은행 동 예금하다 명 둑, 제방	Everyone should have a bank account. 누구나 은행 계좌를 가지고 있어야 한다.
552	**clear** [kliər]	형 알아듣기 쉬운, 분명한 동 치우다	Look at the clear sky! 깨끗한 하늘을 보라!
553	**ear** [iər]	명 귀, 청각 명 경청, 주의	Please tell me in my ear. 내 귀에 대고 이야기 해 주세요.
554	**garden** [gá:rdn]	명 뜰, 정원	I want to live in a garden house. 나는 정원이 있는 집에서 살고싶다.
555	**just** [dʒʌst]	부 ~하는 바로, 그 순간에 형 공정한	She's just arrived. 그녀는 방금 도착했다.
556	**morning** ['mɔːrnɪŋ]	명 새벽, 아침, 오전	It was raining this morning. 오늘 아침에는 비가오고 있었다.
557	**poem** [póuəm]	명 시	She read the poem aloud. 그녀는 그 시를 큰 소리로 읽었다.
558	**serve** [sə:rv]	동 제공하다, 돌아가다	What time do you serve dinner? 저녁식사는 언제 제공하나요?
559	**support** [səpó:rt]	동 지원하다, 지지하다	I support you forever. 나는 너를 영원히 지지한다.
560	**week** [wi:k]	명 주, 일주일	It rained all week. 일주일 내내 비가 왔다.

bank
Everyone should have a bank account.

clear
Look at the clear sky!

ear
Please tell me in my ear.

garden
I want to live in a garden house.

just
She's just arrived.

morning
It was raining this morning.

poem
She read the poem aloud.

serve
What time do you serve dinner?

support
I support you forever.

week
It rained all week.

561	**bar** [ba:r]	명 막대기 명 술집(바)	The gorilla rattled the bars of its cage. 고릴라가 철창살들을 덜컹거렸다.
562	**client** [kláiənt]	명 의뢰인, 고객	I had lunch with my client today. 오늘 점심은 고객과 같이 했다.
563	**early** [ə́:rli]	형 빠른, 이른	Sleep early and get up early. 빨리 자고 일찍 일어나서
564	**gas** [gæs]	명 가스, 기체	The house is heated by gas. 이 집은 난방을 가스로 한다.
565	**keep** [ki:p]	동 ~유지하다, ~계속하다, ~있게하다.	Please keep me a seat. 제발 내 자리를 남겨 둬.
566	**most** [moust]	한, 대 대부분(의) 부 가장	I like most vegetables. 나는 대부분의 야채를 좋아한다.
567	**point** [pɔint]	명 의견, 주장 동 가리키다	My point is simple. 나의 핵심은 간단하다.
568	**set** [set]	동 (특정한 위치에) 놓다 명 세트, (두 개 이상의 물건으로 구성된) 형 계획된, 정해진	Shall we have the set menu? 우리 세트메뉴로 먹을까?
569	**sure** [ʃuər]	형 확실히, 확신하는 부 그럼	He sure looked unhappy. 그는 정말 불행에 보였다.
570	**weight** [weit]	명 무게, 체중	She is trying to lose weight. 그녀는 체중을 줄이려고 노력중이다.

단어와 문장을 따라 쓰세요.

bar
The gorilla rattled the bars of its cage.

client
I had lunch with my client today.

early
Sleep early and get up early.

gas
The house is heated by gas.

keep
Please keep me a seat.

most
I like most vegetables.

point
My point is simple.

set
Shall we have the set menu?

sure
He sure looked unhappy.

weight
She is trying to lose weight.

571	**base** [beis]	명 기초, ~ 맨 아래 동 ~근거를 두다	What do you base it on? 그 근간은 무엇입니까?
572	**climb** [klaɪm]	동 오르다, 올라가다	She attempted to climb the wall. 그녀는 벽 오르기를 시도했다.
573	**earth** [ə:rθ]	명 지구, 세상 동 접지하다	The earth moves around the sun. 지구는 태양의 주위를 돈다.
574	**gate** [geit]	명 문, 출입구, 게이트	We waited for the train at Gate 5. 우리는 5번 게이트에서 열차를 기다렸다.
575	**kept** [kept]	동 keep의 과거·과거분사 형 유지	He kept on talking. 그는 계속해서 말을 했다.
576	**mother** [mʌðər]	명 어머니 동 보살피다, 돌보다.	Her mother was a lovely woman. 그녀의 어머니는 무척 사랑스러운 분이셨다.
577	**poor** [puər]	형 가난한, 빈곤한	Poor is not a sin. 가난한 것은 죄가 아니다.
578	**settle** [sétl]	동 해결하다, 합의보다, 결산하다.	We settle accounts in December. 우리는 12월에 결산한다.
579	**surface** [sə́:rfis]	명 표면, 지면, 수면 동 수면으로 올라오다	The surface of ice is smooth. 얼음의 표면은 매끄럽다.
580	**well** [wel]	부 잘, 좋게, 제대로 형 건강한, 몸이 좋은	She plays quite well. 그녀는 운동을 잘한다.

base
What do you base it on?

climb
She attempted to climb the wall.

earth
The earth moves around the sun.

gate
We waited for the train at Gate 5.

kept
He kept on talking.

mother
Her mother was a lovely woman.

poor
Poor is not a sin.

settle
We settle accounts in December.

surface
The surface of ice is smooth.

well
She plays quite well.

581	**basic** [béisik]	형 기본적인, 기초적인	Home is the basis of a safe life. 집은 안전한 삶의 기본이다.
582	**clock** [klak]	명 시계 동 기록하다	I set the alarm clock for 6 o'clock. 나는 알람 시간을 6시에 맞췄다.
583	**ease** [iːz]	명 편안함, 안락함.	I feel at ease here. 나는 이곳에서 편안함을 느낀다.
584	**gather** [gǽðər]	동 모으다, 모이다.	Bees will gather for flowers. 벌들은 꽃을 찾아 모일 것이다.
585	**key** [kiː]	명 열쇠, 키, 비결	The key didn't fit and I couldn't open the door. 열쇠가 맞지 않아서 문을 열 수 없었다.
586	**motion** [móuʃən]	명 운동, 움직임, 흔들림	Show me again in slow motion. 느린 동작으로 다시 보여주세요.
587	**port** [pɔːrt]	명 항구, 항만, 무역항 명 피난처, 휴식처	The ship steered into port. 그 배가 항구로 들어왔다.
588	**several** [sévərəl]	한, 대 (몇)몇의	She has been in several TV dramas. 그녀는 몇 개의 TV 드라마에 출연했다.
589	**surprise** [sərpráiz]	명 놀라움 동 놀라게 하다	There was surprise news in the newspaper. 신문에 놀라운 뉴스가 실렸다.
590	**went** [went]	동 go의 과거	She went into the house. 그녀는 그 집으로 들어갔다.

단어와 문장을 따라 쓰세요.

basic
Home is the basis of a safe life.

clock
I set the alarm clock for 6 o'clock.

ease
I feel at ease here.

gather
Bees will gather for flowers.

key
The key didn't fit and I couldn't open the door.

motion
Show me again in slow motion.

port
The ship steered into port.

several
She has been in several TV dramas.

surprise
There was surprise news in the newspaper.

went
She went into the house.

591	**basketball** [bǽskitbɔ̀:l]	명 농구, 농구공	Basketball is a popular sport in the United States. 농구는 미국에서 인기 있는 스포츠다.
592	**close** [klouz]	동 닫다, 덮다. 형 가까운	What time does the bank close? 은행이 몇시에 문을 닫죠?
593	**east** [i:st]	명 동쪽, 동부	Dokdo is located on the East Sea. 독도는 동해에 위치해 있다.
594	**gave** [geiv]	동 give의 과거	I gave all of them to him. 나는 그에게 모든 것을 주었다.
595	**kill** [kil]	동 죽이다, 목숨을 빼앗다	The drug can kill the virus. 그 약은 바이러스를 죽일 수 있다.
596	**mount** [maunt]	동 시작하다, 증가하다.	We will mount a general attack. 우리는 총 공격을 시작할 것이다.
597	**pose** [pouz]	명 자세 동 ~ 제기하다.	I pose you the same question. 당신에게 같은 문제를 제기하고 있어요.
598	**shall** [ʃəl]	조 제의·제안·조언 요청	What shall we have for dinner? 저녁으로 뭘 먹을까?
599	**swim** [swim]	동 수영하다, 헤엄치다	Even in winter, I sometimes swim. 겨울에도 나는 가끔 수영을 한다.
600	**west** [west]	명 서쪽, 서양	The sun was sinking in the west. 해가 서쪽으로 지고 있었다.

basketball
Basketball is a popular sport in the United States.

close
What time does the bank close?

east
Dokdo is located on the East Sea.

gave
I gave all of them to him.

kill
The drug can kill the virus.

mount
We will mount a general attack.

pose
I pose you the same question.

shall
What shall we have for dinner?

swim
Even in winter, I sometimes swim.

west
The sun was sinking in the west.

A 주어진 문장에 맞는 단어를 보기에서 찾아 문장을 완성하세요.

❶ He'll be _____ on Monday. 원 위치로, 되돌아서

❷ He lives to the west of the _____. 도시, 시

❸ No one is _____ from birth. 불쾌, 나쁜

❹ The goods exported were made a _____. 요구하다, 주장하다

❺ Yoga is important to _____ your body. 균형

❻ She works hard in _____. 학급, 수업

❼ Who is kicking the _____? 공

❽ The _____ is noisy when it's time to rest. 교실

❾ The _____ was not good at playing. 악단, 밴드

❿ You have to wash it _____ every day. 깨끗한, 깔끔한

> **bad   claim   city   classroom   class   ball   clean   back   band   balance**

B 해석을 보고 빈칸에 해당되는 단어를 보기에서 찾아 적으세요.

❶ _____ the 2000s 2000년대에

   _____ the past one month 지난 한 달 동안

❷ _____ hated the other. 그 둘은 서로를 미워했다.

   _____ one 각자

❸ a piece of _____ 과일 한 개

   grow _____ 과수를 재배하다.

❹ the _____ season 건기

   a _____ voice 건조한 목소리

❺ _____ teeth 앞니

   We had seats in the _____ row. 우리는 좌석이 앞줄에 있었다.

❻ a _____ bottle of wine 한 병 가득 든 포도주

   My heart is _____. 가슴이 벅차다.

❼ a _____ of chance/skill 운/기술이 좌우하는 게임

   a called _____ 중단 경기, 콜드 게임

> **game   during   front   fruit   each   dry   full**

C   보기에 주어진 단어의 설명입니다. 해당되는 단어를 찾아 적으세요.

❶   ~ A and B (together/up) 연결하다   _____

❷   잠깐, 잠시   _____

❸   (일 년 열두 달 중) 달, 월 (calendar month)   _____

❹   (큰) 기쁨, 환희 (유의어 delight)   _____

❺   (바닥을 차며) 뛰다, 점프하다   _____

❻   저널리스트, (신문·방송·잡지사의) 기자   _____

❼   더 많은 수[양]의   _____

| moment | joy | more | join | jump | journalist | month |

D   주어진 해석에 맞는 영어단어로 퍼즐을 완성하세요.

Across

4. 제안하다, 추천하다
6. 행성
7. 깨끗한

Down

1. ~하는 동안
2. 앞면, 앞쪽
3. 잠깐, 잠시
5. 공
6. 식물, 공장

A 주어진 문장에 맞는 단어를 보기에서 찾아 문장을 완성하세요.

❶ Everyone should have a _____ account. 은행

❷ Look at the _____ sky! 깔끔한, 맑은

❸ The gorilla rattled the _____ of its cage. 철창살

❹ I had lunch with my _____ today. 의뢰인, 고객

❺ What do you _____ it on? 기초, 근거

❻ She attempted to _____ the wall. 오르다, 올라가다

❼ Home is the _____ of a safe life. 기반, 근거

❽ I set the alarm _____ for 6 o'clock. 시계

❾ _____ is a popular sport in the United States. 농구

❿ What time does the bank _____? 닫다

| bars | client | clear | basketball | bank | close | climb | basis | base | clock |

B 해석을 보고 빈칸에 해당되는 단어를 보기에서 찾아 적으세요.

❶ the _____ morning 이른 아침

Mozart's _____ works 모차르트의 초기 작품들

❷ to _____ wild flowers 야생화를 꺾어 모으다

_____ experience 경험을 쌓다

❸ the planet _____ 지구라는 행성

the whole _____ 전 세계 사람

❹ a front/back _____ 앞/뒤뜰

_____ flowers/plants 정원의 꽃/초목

❺ a _____ explosion/leak 가스 폭발/누출

a _____ attack 독가스 공격

❻ Which way is _____? 어느 쪽이 동쪽이에요?

The sun rises in the _____. 태양은 동쪽에서 뜬다.

❼ an _____ infection 귓병

| gas | east | garden | gather | early | ear | earth |

C 보기에 주어진 단어의 설명입니다. 해당되는 단어를 찾아 적으세요.

1. (특정한 상태위치를) 유지하다 _____

2. 최대[최고]의, 가장 많음 _____

3. 운동, 움직임, 흔들림 _____

4. '정확히'라는 뜻의 딱 _____

5. (…을 조직하여) 시작하다 (유의어 arrange) _____

6. 아침, 오전(잠자리에서 일어난 시각부터 점심때까지) _____

7. 죽이다, 목숨을 빼앗다 _____

| most | just | kill | keep | motion | morning | mount |

D 주어진 해석에 맞는 영어단어로 퍼즐을 완성하세요.

Across

2. 모으다, 모이다
5. 놀라움
7. 뜰, 정원
9. 운동, 움직임

Down

1. 농구
3. 표면, 지면
4. 아침, 오전
6. 무게, 체중
8. 의견, 가리키다

601	**bat** [bæt]	몡 방망이, 배트 몡 박쥐	The pitcher's ball is too fast to hit with a bat. 투수의 공이 너무 빨라 방망이로 칠 수 없다.
602	**clothe** [klouð]	통 옷을입다.	It will clothe you well. 옷을 잘 입힐 것이다.
603	**eat** [i:t]	통 먹다, 식사하다.	Would you like something to eat? 뭐 좀 드시겠어요?
604	**general** ['dʒenrəl]	혱 보통의, 일반적인	I use the word in a general sense. 나는 이 말을 보통의 뜻으로 쓴다.
605	**kind** [kaind]	혱 친절한, 다정한 몡 종류, 유형	Thank you for your kind invitation. 친절하게 초대해 주셔서 감사합니다.
606	**mountain** [máuntən]	몡 산	The mountain valley is very deep. 그 산의 계곡은 매우 깊다.
607	**position** [pəzíʃən]	몡 위치, 자리	I'm not in a position to decide. 내가 결정할 위치가 아니다.
608	**shape** [ʃeip]	몡 모양, 형태	You are in fine shape. 너는 건강해 보인다.
609	**syllable** [síləbl]	몡 음절	The accent comes on the first syllable. 첫 음절에 악센트가 있다.
610	**what** [hwət]	때 (의문문)무엇 때 (감탄문) 정말	What do you work? 직업이 무엇입니까?

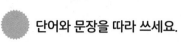

bat

The pitcher's ball is too fast to hit with a bat.

clothe

It will clothe you well.

eat

Would you like something to eat?

general

I use the word in a general sense.

kind

Thank you for your kind invitation.

mountain

The mountain valley is very deep.

position

I'm not in a position to decide.

shape

You are in fine shape.

syllable

The accent comes on the first syllable.

what

What do you work?

611	**beach** [bi:ʧ]	명 해변, 바닷가	I ran along the beach with my dog. 강아지와 함께 해변을 달렸다.
612	**cloud** [klaud]	명 구름, 형 흐리다	It was beginning to cloud over. 날이 점점 흐려지고 있었다.
613	**edge** [edʒ]	명 끝, 가장자리, 모서리	I hit the table edge on. 나는 테이블 가장자리에 부딪쳤다.
614	**gentle** [dʒéntl]	형 온화한, 순한; 조용한, 조심스러운 부 다정하게, 부드럽게, 완만하게	He was a gentle, insightful soul. 그는 온화하고 통찰력 있는 사람이다.
615	**king** [kiŋ]	명 왕, 국왕	He was true to the king. 그는 왕에게 충성했다.
616	**mouth** [mauθ]	명 입	My mouth got dirty. 입이 더러워 졌다.
617	**possible** [pásəbl]	형 가능한, 있을 수 있는	If possible I'd like to go with you. 가능하다면, 너와 함께 가고 싶다.
618	**share** [ʃɛər]	동 함께쓰다, 공유하다.	I decided to share a room with my close friend. 친한 친구와 방을 같이 사용하기로 했다.
619	**symbol** [símbəl]	명 상징 부호	It is a symbol of my victory. 그것은 나의 승리의 상징이다
620	**wheel** [hwi:l]	명 바퀴, 핸들, 돌림판	The world is a wheel. 세상은 수레 바퀴와 같다.

beach
I ran along the beach with my dog.

cloud
It was beginning to cloud over.

edge
I hit the table edge on.

gentle
He was a gentle, insightful soul.

king
He was true to the king.

mouth
My mouth got dirty.

possible
If possible I'd like to go with you.

share
I decided to share a room with my close friend.

symbol
It is a symbol of my victory.

wheel
The world is a wheel.

621	**bear** [ber]	통 참다, 견디다	How much pain can you bear? 얼마나 많은 고통을 참을 수 있나요?
622	**coast** [koust]	명 해안	We walked along the coast. 우리는 해안을 따라 걸었다.
623	**editor** [édətər]	명 편집자, 편집장	The editor removed the article. 편집자가 기사를 제거했다.
624	**German** [dʒɔ́:rmən]	명 독일인, 독일 사람	He majored in German at the university. 그는 대학에서 독일어를 전공했다.
625	**knew** [njuː]	know의 과거	I knew where he was hiding. 나는 그가 어디 숨었는지 알고있었다.
626	**move** [muːv]	통 움직이다, 바뀌다, 달라지다	I can't move my fingers. 나는 손가락을 움직일 수 없다.
627	**post** [poust]	명 우편, 우편물	Please bring the mail to the post office. 우편물을 우체국에 가져다 주세요.
628	**sharp** [ʃaːrp]	형 날카로운, 뾰족한, 예리한	He has very sharp eyes. 그는 매우 날카로운 눈을 가졌다.
629	**system** [sístəm]	명 체계, 시스템, 장치	The system doesn't work! 시스템이 작동하지 않아!
630	**when** [hwən]	부 언제, 때	When does the train go? 기차는 언제 떠나나요?

bear

How much pain can you bear?

coast

We walked along the coast.

editor

The editor removed the article.

German

He majored in German at the university.

knew

I knew where he was hiding.

move

I can't move my fingers.

post

Please bring the mail to the post office.

sharp

He has very sharp eyes.

system

The system doesn't work!

when

When does the train go?

631	**beat** [biːt]	통 이기다, 억제하다.	She beat me at chess. 그녀가 체스에서 나를 이겼다.
632	**coat** [kout]	명 외투 코트 통 덮다	He was wearing a new coat. 그는 새로운 외투를 입고 있었다.
633	**effect** [ifékt]	명 영향, 결과, 효과	This gas causes a greenhouse effect. 이 가스는 온실 효과를 일으킨다.
634	**get** [get]	통 얻다, 구하다, 마련하다 자 자동사 (장소·지위·상태) 이르다, 도달하다.	You can get a bus back. 돌아가는 버스를 타면됩니다.
635	**know** [nou]	통 알다, 알고 있다	I know things you don't know. 나는 네가 모르는 것들을 알고있다.
636	**much** [mʌtʃ]	부 매우, 너무, 정말, 많이	You worry too much. 너는 걱정을 너무 많이 해.
637	**pound** [paund]	명 (화폐단위, 중량단위) 파운드	They cost one dollar a pound. 그 가격은 파운드 당 1달러이다.
638	**she** [ʃi]	대 그녀	She said that she couldn't come. 그녀는 올 수 없다고 말했다.
639	**table** [téibl]	명 식탁, 테이블, 탁자	Keys are on the table. 열쇠들이 테이블 위에 있다.
640	**where** [hwɛər]	부 어디에, 어디로, 어디에서	Where did you buy that coat? 그 코트는 어디에서 샀나요?

beat

She beat me at chess.

coat

He was wearing a new coat.

effect

This gas causes a greenhouse effect.

get

You can get a bus back.

know

I know things you don't know.

much

You worry too much.

pound

They cost one dollar a pound.

she

She said that she couldn't come.

table

Keys are on the table.

where

Where did you buy that coat?

641	**beauty** [bjúːti]	몡 미인, 아름다운 것	That last goal was a beauty! 그 마지막 골은 정말 멋있엇다.
642	**cold** [kould]	형 추운, 차가운	The soup was stone cold. 그 수프는 얼음처럼 다 식었다.
643	**egg** [eg]	몡 달걀, 계란	I eat an egg at breakfast. 나는 아침식사때 달걀을 하나 먹는다.
644	**gift** [gift]	몡 선물, 기증품	What do you want as a gift? 선물로 무엇을 원하니?
645	**lady** [léidi]	몡 여자 분, 여성, 숙녀	The lady is waiting for you. 어떤 숙녀분이 당신을 기다리고 있습니다.
646	**multiply** [mʌ́ltəplài]	통 곱하다, 증가시키다.	Multiply 2 and 7 together and you get 14. 2와 7을 곱하면 14가 된다.
647	**power** ['pauə(r)]	몡 권력, 정권, 힘	That's not in my power. 그것은 내 능력 밖의 일이다.
648	**sheet** [ʃiːt]	몡 시트, 한 장	You went as white as a sheet. 당신 얼굴이 창백해 졌다.
649	**tail** [teil]	몡 꼬리 통 미행하다	They use their tail for balance. 그들은 균형을 잡기 위해 꼬리를 사용한다.
650	**whether** [hwéðər]	접 ~인지, ~ 이든	It may be asked whether it is safe. 그것이 안전한지 의문이 든다.

● 단어와 문장을 따라 쓰세요.

beauty

That last goal was a beauty!

cold

The soup was stone cold.

egg

I eat an egg at breakfast.

gift

What do you want as a gift?

lady

The lady is waiting for you.

multiply

Multiply 2 and 7 together and you get 14.

power

That's not in my power.

sheet

You went as white as a sheet.

tail

They use their tail for balance.

whether

It may be asked whether it is safe.

651	**bed** [bed]	통 침대 명 바닥	It's time for bed. 지금은 자야할 시간이다.
652	**collect** [kəlékt]	통 모으다, 수집하다 형 수신자가 부담하는	If you collect five stamps, you'll get a free drink. 도장 5개를 모으면 한 잔 무료이다.
653	**either** [íːðər]	한 대명사 (둘 중)하나, 각각	He doesn't dress well, either. 그는 옷을 잘 입는 것도 아닙니다.
654	**give** [giv]	통 주다, 건네주다.	Give back my glasses. 내 안경을 돌려주세요.
655	**lake** [leik]	명 호수	We sometimes swam in the lake. 우리는 가끔 호수에서 수영을 했다.
656	**museum** [mjuːzíːəm]	명 미술관, 박물관	The museum in Paris must go. 파리에 있는 박물관은 꼭 가봐야 한다.
657	**practice** ['præktɪs]	명 실행, 실천	Practice is the basis of success. 연습이 성공의 기본이다.
658	**shine** [ʃain]	통 빛나다, 반짝이다.	The jewels shine in the light. 보석이 빛에 반짝이다.
659	**take** [teik]	통 가지고 있다. 잡다. 데리고 가다. 명 장면(영화)	I'll take you home. 너의 집까지 데려다 줄께요.
660	**which** [wɪtʃ]	대 (의문문에서) 어느[어떤]	Which one's your favorite? 너는 어느것이 좋니?

bed

It's time for bed.

collect

If you collect five stamps, you'll get a free drink.

either

He doesn't dress well, either.

give

Give back my glasses.

lake

We sometimes swam in the lake.

museum

The museum in Paris must go.

practice

Practice is the basis of success.

shine

The jewels shine in the light.

take

I'll take you home.

which

Which one's your favorite?

661	**bedroom** [bédrù:m]	명 침실, 방	I want to change the color of the bedroom. 침실 색상을 바꾸고 싶다.
662	**colony** [káləni]	명 식민지	The country was once a colony. 그 나라는 한때 식민지 였다.
663	**electric** [iléktrik]	형 전기의, 전기를 이용하는	I saw a lot of electric cars. 나는 전기 자동차를 많이 보았다.
664	**glad** [glæd]	형 고마운	She brought glad tidings. 그녀는 반가운 소식을 가지고 왔었다.
665	**land** [lænd]	명 육지, 땅 동 내려앉다, 착륙하다	This land belongs to me. 이땅은나의 소유이다.
666	**music** [mjú:zik]	명 음악, 곡	I like modern music. 나는 현대 음악을 좋아한다.
667	**prepare** [pripέər]	동 준비하다, 대비하다	I lacked time to prepare. 대비할 시간이 부족했다.
668	**ship** [ʃip]	명 배, 선박	The ship is shaking! 배가 흔들려요.
669	**talk** [tɔ:k]	동 말하다. 논의하다.	Can I talk to you? 나와 이야기 할 수 있을까?
670	**while** [hwail]	명 잠깐, 잠시, 동안 접 ~하는 동안에	I burned my hand while cooking. 요리를 하다가 손에 화상을 입었다.

● 단어와 문장을 따라 쓰세요.

bedroom

I want to change the color of the bedroom.

colony

The country was once a colony.

electric

I saw a lot of electric cars.

glad

She brought glad tidings.

land

This land belongs to me.

music

I like modern music.

prepare

I lacked time to prepare.

ship

The ship is shaking!

talk

Can I talk to you?

while

I burned my hand while cooking.

671	**been** [bin]	동 ~ 했다. 했었다.	She has been to China. 그녀는 중국에 갔다왔다.
672	**color** [kʌlər]	명 색, 색깔. 동 색칠하다	What color is your car? 여러분의 차는 무슨 색이죠?
673	**element** [éləmənt]	명 요소, 성분	What is the element of air? 공기의 요소가 무엇이지?
674	**glass** [glæs]	명 유리, 유리잔	Give me a glass of milk. 우유 한 잔 주세요.
675	**language** [læŋgwidʒ]	명 언어, 말	They communicated in sign language. 그들은 수화로 의사소통 했다.
676	**must** [məst]	조 …해야 하다. ~ 틀림없다. 명 꼭 해야	You must try harder. 너는 더 열심히 일해야한다.
677	**present** [préznt]	형 현재의, 현 , 참석 명 선물	This is a present for you. 너를 위한 선물이야.
678	**shop** [ʃap]	명 가게, 상점	This shop cut under than the others. 이 상점은 다른 가게 보다 싸게 판다.
679	**tall** [tɔːl]	형 키가 큰, 높은	He is tall and handsome. 그는 키가 크고 잘생겼다.
680	**white** [wait]	형 흰, 흰색의 명 흰색	She painted the door white. 그녀는 문을 흰색으로 칠했다.

been

She has been to China.

color

What color is your car?

element

What is the element of air?

glass

Give me a glass of milk.

language

They communicated in sign language.

must

You must try harder.

present

This is a present for you.

shop

This shop cut under than the others.

tall

He is tall and handsome.

white

She painted the door white.

681	**before** [bifɔ́ːr]	전 ~ 앞에 접 ~ 하기전에	He arrived before me. 그는 나보다 먼저 도착했다.
682	**come** [kʌm]	통 오다.	Come into the house. 집으로 들어와.
683	**else** [els]	부 다른	Who else knows about this? 다른 누가 이것에 대해 알고 있나요?
684	**global** [glóubəl]	형 세계적인, 지구의	Samsung is a global company. 삼성은 세계적인 기업이다.
685	**large** [laːrdʒ]	형 규모가 큰, 양이 많은 형 광범위한	He was holding a large box. 그가 큰 상자를 들고 있었다.
686	**my** [maɪ]	한 나의, 내	My father appeared in my dream last night. 나의 아버지가 어제 밤 꿈에 나타나셨다.
687	**press** [pres]	명 신문, 언론 통 누르다.	Press cancel to select again. 다시 선택하려면 취소를 누르세요.
688	**short** [ʃɔːrt]	형 짧은 부 ~이 부족하다.	Short skirts are in again. 짧은 치마가 다시 유행이다.
689	**teach** [tiːtʃ]	통 가르치다.	Teach her some work. 그녀에게 일을 좀 가르치세요.
690	**who** [huː]	대 (의문문에서) 누구	Who is your favorite author? 당신이 좋아하는 작가는 누구인가요?

단어와 문장을 따라 쓰세요.

before
He arrived before me.

come
Come into the house.

else
Who else knows about this?

global
Samsung is a global company.

large
He was holding a large box.

my
My father appeared in my dream last night.

press
Press cancel to select again.

short
Short skirts are in again.

teach
Teach her some work.

who
Who is your favorite author?

691	**began** [bigǽn]	begin의 과거	A light rain began to fall. 보슬비가 내리기 시작했다.
692	**common** ['kɑːmən]	형 공동의, 공통의, 흔한	It's not a word in common usage. 그 단어는 흔히 사용되는 단어가 아니다.
693	**emergency** [imɔ́ːrdʒənsi]	명 비상	It's a big fire. It's an emergency. 큰 불이 났다. 지금 비상이다.
694	**go** [gou]	동 가다.	It's time to go now. 이제 가야할 시간이다.
695	**last** [læst]	부 맨 끝에, 마지막에 한정사 마지막의	It happened late last year. 그것은 작년말에 일어났다.
696	**name** [neim]	명 이름, 성명 동 이름을 지어주다	What is your name? 당신 이름이 뭐죠?
697	**pretty** [príti]	형 매력적인, 이쁜 부 어느 정도, 꽤	My parents bought me a pretty dress. 부모님이 예쁜 드레스를 사 주셨다.
698	**should** [ʃəd]	조 …해야 한다, ~ 일것이다.	We should be there by noon. 우리는 정오까지 그곳에 가야한다.
699	**team** [tiːm]	명 팀(스포츠 경기), 단체	I have a baseball team that cheers. 나는 응원하는 야구 팀이 있다.
700	**whole** [houl]	형 전체, 모든 명 완전체	I've sold the whole lot. 나는 전부를 다 팔았다.

began
A light rain began to fall.

common
It's not a word in common usage.

emergency
It's a big fire.   It's an emergency.

go
It's time to go now.

last
It happened late last year.

name
What is your name?

pretty
My parents bought me a pretty dress.

should
We should be there by noon.

team
I have a baseball team that cheers.

whole
I've sold the whole lot.

A 주어진 문장에 맞는 단어를 보기에서 찾아 문장을 완성하세요.

① The pitcher's ball is too fast to hit with a _____ . 배트, 치다

② It will _____ you well. 옷을 입히다, 옷을 마련해 주다

③ I ran along the _____ with my dog. 해변, 바닷가

④ It was beginning to _____ over. 구름

⑤ How much pain can you _____ ? 참다, 견디다

⑥ Please bring the mail to the _____ office. 우편, 우편물

⑦ She _____ me at chess. 이기다

⑧ That last goal was a _____ ! 아름다운, 미인

⑨ The soup was stone _____ . 추운, 차가운

⑩ That's not in my _____ . 힘, 능력

| cloud | cold | post | beauty | power | bear | beat | bat | clothe | beach |

B 해석을 보고 빈칸에 해당되는 단어를 보기에서 찾아 적으세요.

① Stand the coin on its _____ . 동전을 모서리로 세워라.

Be careful, it has a sharp _____ . 조심해. 그건 날이 날카로워.

② I don't _____ meat. 나는 고기[육류]를 안 먹는다.

What did you _____ for lunch? 점심에 무엇을 먹었나요?

③ a quiet and _____ man 조용하고 온화한 남자

Be _____ with her! 그녀에게 다정하게 대해요!

④ the sports/financial/fashion, etc. _____ 스포츠/경제/패션 등의 부문 편집장

a chief _____ 편집장

⑤ a free _____ for every reader 모든 독자에게 드리는 무료 선물

a Christmas _____ 크리스마스 선물.

⑥ a boiled _____ 삶은 달걀

_____ yolks/whites 달걀노른자/흰자

| gentle | gift | edge | egg | editor | eat |

C

보기에 주어진 단어의 설명입니다. 해당되는 단어를 찾아 적으세요.

① 알다, 알고 있다 _____

② (몸 등을) 움직이다 _____

③ 많은, 많음 _____

④ 종류, 유형 _____

⑤ 여자 분, 여성 _____

⑥ ~ A and B 곱하다 _____

⑦ (사람·사물을 통제할 수 있는) 힘 _____

> move　　power　　lady　　much　　know　　kind　　multiply

D

주어진 해석에 맞는 영어단어로 퍼즐을 완성하세요.

Across

2. 구름
4. 영향, 결과
5. 움직이다
6. 상징
8. 해안
9. 식탁, 탁자

Down

1. 가장자리, 모서리
3. 보통의, 일반적인
6. 모양, 형태
7. 우편

A 주어진 문장에 맞는 단어를 보기에서 찾아 문장을 완성하세요.

① It's time for _____ . 침대

② If you _____ five stamps, you'll get a free drink. 모으다

③ I want to change the color of the _____ . 침실

④ The country was once a _____ . 식민지

⑤ She has _____ to China. ~ 이다. ~이었다

⑥ What _____ is your car? 색

⑦ He arrived _____ me. ~전에, ~ 앞에

⑧ _____ into the house. 오다

⑨ A light rain _____ to fall. 시작되다

⑩ It's not a word in _____ usage. 흔한, 공통의

> **bedroom before bed colony began been color common collect Come**

B 해석을 보고 빈칸에 해당되는 단어를 보기에서 찾아 적으세요.

① I don't know _____ . 어느 쪽도 모른다.
You can take _____ book. (둘 중) 어느 책이든 가져라.

② _____ me a call tomorrow. 내일 나한테 전화해.
_____ a person one's blessings ~을 축복해 주다

③ I have to _____ to the hospital. 난 입원해야 한다.
_____ for a drive[walk, swim] 드라이브[산책, 수영]하러 가다

④ _____ issues 세계적인 쟁점들
the _____ market 세계 시장

⑤ look in the _____ 거울을 보다
The vegetables are grown under _____ . 그 채소들은 온실에서 자란다.

⑥ The _____ will be off tomorrow. 내일은 정전이 될 것이다
an _____ violin 전기 바이올린

⑦ I am _____ of it. 그거, 기쁜 일이다.
I'm very _____ to see you. 만나 뵙게 되어 매우 기쁩니다.

> **go   electric   glad   global   either   glass   give**

C 보기에 주어진 단어의 설명입니다. 해당되는 단어를 찾아 적으세요.

① 육지, 뭍, 땅 _____

② (특정 국가·지역의) 언어 _____

③ (규모가) 큰; (양이) 많은 _____

④ 이름, 성명, 성함 _____

⑤ 박물관, 미술관 _____

⑥ ~해야 하다 _____

⑦ 음악, 곡 _____

| large | must | land | museum | name | music | language |

D 주어진 해석에 맞는 영어단어로 퍼즐을 완성하세요.

Across

1. 식민지
6. 큰, 양이 많은
7. 언론, 신문
9. 모으다, 수집하다
10. 미술관, 박물관

Down

2. 호수
3. 색, 색깔
4. 세계적인, 지구의
5. 음악, 곡
8. 현재의, 참석

701	**begin** [bigín]	통 시작하다. 명 시작	When does the concert begin? 콘서트는 언제 시작하죠?
702	**communication** [kəˌmjuːnɪˈkeɪʃn]	명 의사소통, 연락	Communication is accomplished in various ways. 의사 소통이 다양한 방식으로 이루어진다.
703	**empty** [émpti]	형 비어 있는, 빈	There are many empty places in the library. 도서관에 빈 자리가 많다.
704	**gold** [gould]	명 금 형 금빛	They were mining for gold. 그들은 금을 캐고 있었다.
705	**late** [leit]	형 늦은, 늦께	I was late for a class. 나는 수업시간에 지각했다.
706	**nation** [néiʃən]	명 국가, 국민	Korea is the only single nation. 한국은 유일한 단일민족 국가이다.
707	**print** [prɪnt]	통 인쇄하다, 프린트를 하다	It became easier to print at home. 집에서 인쇄하는 것이 쉬워졌다.
708	**shoulder** [ʃóuldər]	명 어깨	I saw her over his shoulder. 그의 어깨 넘어 그녀를 보았다.
709	**teeth** [tiːθ]	tooth의 복수	Two teeth should be pulled out because of the cavities. 충치때무에 치아 두개를 뽑아야 한다.
710	**whose** [huːz]	한, 대 누구의	Whose passport copy do you need? 누구 여권 사본이 필요하세요?

단어와 문장을 따라 쓰세요.

begin
When does the concert begin?

communication
Communication is accomplished in various ways.

empty
There are many empty places in the library.

gold
They were mining for gold.

late
I was late for a class.

nation
Korea is the only single nation.

print
It became easier to print at home.

shoulder
I saw her over his shoulder.

teeth
Two teeth should be pulled out because of the cavities.

whose
Whose passport copy do you need?

711	**behind** [biháind]	튀 뒤에, 뒤떨어져	The sun went behind a cloud. 해가 구름뒤에로 들어갔다.
712	**company** [kʌ́mpəni]	명 회사, 단체	The company was his first job. 그 회사는 그의 첫번째 직장이었다.
713	**end** [end]	명 (사건, 활동, 이야기) 끝 동 끝나다, 끝내다, 끝을 맺다.	How does the story end? 그 이야기는 어떻게 끝나니?
714	**gone** [gɔ(:)n]	형 떠난, 가버린	She's gone for some milk. 그녀는 우유를 가지러 갔다.
715	**laugh** [læf]	동 웃다 명 웃음소리	He always makes me laugh. 그는 항상 나를 웃게 만든다.
716	**natural** [nǽtʃərəl]	형 자연 발생적인, 정상적인, 당연한	He has natural curly hair. 그는 원래부터 곱슬머리이다.
717	**probable** [prábəbl]	형 ~이 있을거 같은, 개연성 있는	A storm is probable today. 오늘 태풍이 올 것 같다.
718	**shout** [ʃaut]	동 외치다, 소리치다.	When she appeared, people began to shout. 그녀가 나타나자 사람들이 소리치기 시작했다.
719	**tell** [tel]	동 알리다, 전하다, 말하다	Tell me all your news. 너의 모든 소식을 말해죠.
720	**why** [hwai]	튀 왜, 무엇 때문에 감 아니	Why did you wave at her? 왜 그녀를 보고 손을 흔들었니?

behind

The sun went behind a cloud.

company

The company was his first job.

end

How does the story end?

gone

She's gone for some milk.

laugh

He always makes me laugh.

natural

He has natural curly hair.

probable

A storm is probable today.

shout

When she appeared, people began to shout.

tell

Tell me all your news.

why

Why did you wave at her?

721	**believe** [bilíːv]	통 믿다, 가능하다고 생각하다.	We believe that the earth is round. 우리는 지구가 둥글다는 것을 믿는다.
722	**compare** [kəmpɛ́ər]	통 비교하다, 필적하다, 비유하다	It is very unpleasant to compare with him. 그와 비교하는 것은 매우 불쾌하다.
723	**enemy** [énəmi]	명 적, 적군	I will think of you as an enemy after this time. 이 시간 이후 너를 적으로 생각하겠다.
724	**good** [gʊd]	형 즐거운, 기쁜, 좋은	She is a very good man. 그녀는 매우 좋은 사람이다.
725	**law** [lɔː]	명 법, 법률	The law must be revised. 그 법은 개정되어야 한다.
726	**nature** ['neɪtʃə(r)]	명 천성, 본성, 자연	He is very sensitive by nature. 그는 천성이 아주 예민하다.
727	**problem** [prábləm]	명 문제 형 문제를 일으키다	He's got a drinking problem. 그는 음주 문제가 있다.
728	**show** [ʃou]	통 보여 주다, 증명하다. 명 (극장, 공연) 쇼	The show is going outlive. 그 쇼는 생방송으로 진행되고 있다.
729	**temperature** [temprətʃə]	명 온도, 기온	The temperature of the room is going up. 방의 온도가 올라가고 있다.
730	**wide** [waid]	형 넓은, 너른	The plains are wide and dry. 평원은 넓고 메마르다.

believe

We believe that the earth is round.

compare

It is very unpleasant to compare with him.

enemy

I will think of you as an enemy after this time.

good

She is a very good man.

law

The law must be revised.

nature

He is very sensitive by nature.

problem

He's got a drinking problem.

show

The show is going outlive.

temperature

The temperature of the room is going up.

wide

The plains are wide and dry.

731	**bell** [bel] 벨	몡 벨, 벨소리	The bell rang to tell me the time. 종을 울려 시간을 알려주었다.
732	**complain** [kəmpléin]	통 불평하다.	Many people complain about this product. 많은 사람이 이 제품에 대해 불평한다.
733	**energy** [énərdʒi]	몡 힘, 에너지, 동력 자원	She's always full of energy. 그녀는 항상 활기가 넘친다.
734	**got** [gat]	통 get의 과거·과거분사	She's got three children. 그녀에게는 아이가 셋 있다.
735	**lay** [lei]	통 눕다 타 눕히다.	A blanket of snow lay on the ground. 눈이 땅위에 덮혀 있다.
736	**near** [niər]	혱 (거리, 시간) 가까운 튄 (거리상으로) 가까이	His house is very near. 그의 집은 아주 가깝다.
737	**process** [práses]	몡 과정	Some changes happened in the process. 그 과정에서 몇가지 변화가 생겼다.
738	**side** [said]	몡 한쪽, 한편	She was lying on his side. 그녀는 옆으로 누워 있었다.
739	**test** [test]	몡 시험, 테스트	She failed his driving test. 그녀는 운전면허 시험에 떨어졌다.
740	**wife** [waif]	몡 아내, 처, 부인	His wife is always friendly. 그의 아내는 언제나 친절하다.

bell

The bell rang to tell me the time.

complain

Many people complain about this product.

energy

She's always full of energy.

got

She's got three children.

lay

A blanket of snow lay on the ground.

near

His house is very near.

process

Some changes happened in the process.

side

She was lying on his side.

test

She failed his driving test.

wife

His wife is always friendly.

741	**best** [best]	휑 가장 행복한[즐거운], 최고의 분 가장	English is my best subject. 영어는 내가 가장 잘하는 과목이다.
742	**complete** [kəmˈpliːt]	휑 필요한 모든 것이 갖춰진, 완전한	I want to complete it. 나는 이것을 끝내고 싶다.
743	**engine** [éndʒin]	명 엔진, 기관	The engine failed suddenly. 엔진이 갑자기 꺼졌다.
744	**govern** [gʌ́vərn]	동 통치하다, 지배하다.	I don't know how to govern. 나는 통치하는 방법을 모른다.
745	**lead** [liːd]	동 안내하다, (장소)연결하다.	The stairs lead to the second story. 그 계단은 2층으로 연결되어 있다.
746	**necessary** [nesəseri]	휑 필연적인, 불가피한	It is not necessarily necessary. 반드시 필요한 것은 아니다.
747	**produce** [prədjúːs]	동 생산하다, 낳다.	She wanted to produce a new model. 그녀는 새로운 모델을 생산하고 싶었다.
748	**sight** [sait]	명 시력, 보기	He has very good sight. 그는 시력이 매우 좋다.
749	**than** [ðən]	전 ~보다	I'm older than her. 나는 그녀보다 나이가 더 많다.
750	**wild** [waild]	휑 야생의, 자연의	These plants grow wild. 이 식물은 야생에서 자란다.

단어와 문장을 따라 쓰세요.

best

English is my best subject.

complete

I want to complete it.

engine

The engine failed suddenly.

govern

I don't know how to govern.

lead

The stairs lead to the second story.

necessary

It is not necessarily necessary.

produce

She wanted to produce a new model.

sight

He has very good sight.

than

I'm older than her.

wild

These plants grow wild.

751	**better** [bétər]	혱 더 잘 하는 悍 더 잘	Do you have a better solution? 더 좋은 해결책이 있나요?
752	**condition** [kəndíʃən]	명 상태	The player is in the best condition. 그 선수는 최상의 상태이다.
753	**enough** [inʌf]	때 필요한 만큼 되는 수 핸 필요한 만큼의	He has enough money to live on. 그는 먹고 살만큼 충분한 돈이 있다.
754	**graduate** [grǽdʒuət]	명 졸업자	You need credits to graduate. 졸업하려면 학점이 필요하다.
755	**learn** [lɜːrn]	동 배우다, 학습하다	I'd like to learn a new language. 나는 새로운 언어를 배우고 싶다.
756	**neck** [nek]	명 목, 목부분	She tied a scarf around his neck. 그녀는 목에 스카프를 맸다.
757	**product** [prádʌkt]	명 생산물, 상품, 제품	Thank you for using our product. 저희 제품을 이용해 주셔서 감사합니다.
758	**sign** [sain]	명 징후, 조짐, 기색, 흔적 명 표시, 사인	They're looking at the sign. 사람들이 표지판을 보고 있다.
759	**thank** [θæŋk]	동 감사하다, 고마워하다, 감사를 표하다	Thank you for your welcome. 환영해 주셔서 감사합니다.
760	**will** [wəl]	조, 동 [단순미래] …할 [일] 것이다	I will begin again. 나는 다시 시작할 것이다.

better

Do you have a better solution?

condition

The player is in the best condition.

enough

He has enough money to live on.

graduate

You need credits to graduate.

learn

I'd like to learn a new language.

neck

She tied a scarf around his neck.

product

Thank you for using our product.

sign

They're looking at the sign.

thank

Thank you for your welcome.

will

I will begin again.

761	**between** [bitwíːn]	젠 사이, 중간에	He left between five and six o'clock. 그는 5섯와 6섯시 사이에 떠났다.
762	**confirm** [kənfɔ́ːrm]	통 확정하다. 사실임을 보여주다.	Please call me to confirm. 확인 전화 주세요.
763	**enter** [éntər]	통 들어가다, 시작하다 명 입장	Please enter in order. 순서대로 입장해 주세요.
764	**grand** [grænd]	형 웅장한, 장려한	I got the grand prize. 나는 대상을 받았다.
765	**least** [liːst]	부 가장 덜, 최소로 한 가장적은	She reads at least one book a week. 그녀는 적어도 일주일에 한 권의 책을 읽는다.
766	**need** [niːd]	통 (…을) 필요로 하다, ~ 해야한다. 조 (긍정문에서) …할 필 요가 있다	I need a room of my own. 나는 나만의 방이 필요하다.
767	**proper** [prápər]	형 적절한, 제대로 된 명 예의, 예의범절	This is a proper name. 이것은 적절한 이름이다.
768	**silent** [sáilənt]	형 말을 안 하는, 침묵을 지키는, 조용한	The people all began to be silent. 사람들은 모두 침묵하기 시작했다.
769	**that** [ðæˈt]	형 저쪽의, 그쪽의 대 저 사람, 저것	Don't say that. 그렇게 이야기 하지 마라.
770	**win** [win]	통 이기다.	We can win enough. 우리는 충분히 이길 수 있다.

단어와 문장을 따라 쓰세요.

between
He left between five and six o'clock.

confirm
Please call me to confirm.

enter
Please enter in order.

grand
I got the grand prize.

least
She reads at least one book a week.

need
I need a room of my own.

proper
This is a proper name.

silent
The people all began to be silent.

that
Don't say that.

win
We can win enough.

771	**big** [big]	형 치수, 양이 큰 부 크게	I never eat a big dinner. 나는 절대 밥을 많이 안먹는다.
772	**connect** [kənékt]	동 잇다, 연결하다, 이어지다.	I'm trying to connect with you. 연결해 드리겠습니다.
773	**equal** [íːkwəl]	형 평등한, 동일한	We started from an equal position. 우리는 동일한 위치에서 출발했다.
774	**grass** [græs]	명 풀, 잔디	Goats eat grass. 염소는 풀을 먹는다.
775	**leave** [liːv]	동 떠나다	She had to leave in a hurry. 그녀는 급히 떠나야 했다.
776	**negative** [négətiv]	형 부정적, 비관적, 소극적	People's reactions were negative. 사람들의 반응은 부정적이다.
777	**property** [prápərti]	명 재산, 소유물	This park is government property. 이 공원은 정부의 재산입니다.
778	**silver** [sílvər]	명 은, 은동전	He won a silver medal in the high jump. 그는 높이뛰기에서 은메달을 받았다.
779	**their** [ðər]	한 그들의, 그것들의(남성인지 여성인지 모르거나 언급하고싶지 않을때)	Their new album is dynamite. 그들의 새로운 앨범은 강력하다.
780	**wind** [wind]	명 바람	The wind is blowing from the south. 바람이 남쪽에서 불어오고 있다.

big
I never eat a big dinner.

connect
I'm trying to connect with you.

equal
We started from an equal position.

grass
Goats eat grass.

leave
She had to leave in a hurry.

negative
People's reactions were negative.

property
This park is government property.

silver
He won a silver medal in the high jump.

their
Their new album is dynamite.

wind
The wind is blowing from the south.

781	**bike** [baik]	명 자전거, 오토바이	I bought a new mountain bike. 산악 자전거를 새로 구입했다.
782	**consider** [kənsídər]	동 고려하다, ~로 여기다. 명 사려, 숙고	There are too many things to consider in this matter. 이 문제는 고려해야 할 사항이 너무 많다.
783	**equate** [ikwéit]	동 동일시하다	I equate horror to telling a joke. 내게 농담하는 것은 공포와 마찬가지이다.
784	**gray** [grei]	명 회색	They competed in gray uniforms. 그들은 회색 유니폼을 입고 출전했다.
785	**left** [left]	형 왼쪽의, 좌측의	I broke my left leg. 나의 왼쪽 다리가 부러졌다.
786	**neighbor** [néibər]	명 이웃, 옆자리 사람	A near neighbor is better than a distant cousin. 가까운 이웃이 먼 사촌보다 낫다.
787	**protect** [prətékt]	동 보호하다, 지키다	You must protect the weak. 약자를 보호해야 한다.
788	**similar** [símələr]	형 비슷한, 유사한, 닮은	There were many very similar cases. 매우 비슷한 사례들이 많았다.
789	**them** [ðəm]	대 그들에게, 그것들에게	Tell them the news. 그들에게 소식을 전해라.
790	**window** [wíndou]	명 창문, 창	Shall we open the window? 창문을 열까요?

단어와 문장을 따라 쓰세요.

bike

I bought a new mountain bike.

consider

There are too many things to consider in this matter.

equate

I equate horror to telling a joke.

gray

They competed in gray uniforms.

left

I broke my left leg.

neighbor

A near neighbor is better than a distant cousin.

protect

You must protect the weak.

similar

There were many very similar cases.

them

Tell them the news.

window

Shall we open the window?

791	**bird** [bəːrd]	몡 새	A bird sits on the wire. 새 한마리가 전선위에 앉아 있다.
792	**contain** [kəntéin]	통 들어있다. ~ 방지하다.	The pockets contain seeds. 봉지안에 씨앗들이 들어있다.
793	**even** [íːvən]	뷔 …조차도, …(이)라도, …까지도 뷔 (비교급을 강조하여) 훨씬	She didn't even say sorry 그녀는 미안하다는 말조차 하지 않았다.
794	**great** [greit]	휑 큰. 거대한 몡 위대한 (인물을 나타 낼 때)	She is a great talent. 그녀는 재능이 뛰어난 사람이다.
795	**leg** [leg]	몡 다리	He has a weak leg. 그는 다리가 약하다.
796	**never** [névər]	뷔 결코, ~ 않다.	She never drinks alcohol. 그녀는 절대 술을 마시지 않는다.
797	**prove** [pruːv]	통 입증, 증명하다.	Prove me wrong. 내가 틀린 것을 증명해 보시오.
798	**simple** ['sɪmpl]	휑 단순한, 소박한, 간소한	The reason is simple. 그 이유는 간단하다.
799	**then** [ðen]	뷔 그때, 그 다음에, 그리고, 그러더니	Shall we meet at four, then? 우리 그럼 4시에 만날까?
800	**winter** [wíntər]	몡 겨울	I'm going to go skiing this winter. 나는 이번 겨울에 스키를 타러 갈 것이다.

bird

A bird sits on the wire.

contain

The pockets contain seeds.

even

She didn't even say sorry

great

She is a great talent.

leg

He has a weak leg.

never

She never drinks alcohol.

prove

Prove me wrong.

simple

The reason is simple.

then

Shall we meet at four, then?

winter

I'm going to go skiing this winter.

A 주어진 문장에 맞는 단어를 보기에서 찾아 문장을 완성하세요.

① When does the concert _____ ? 시작하다

② _____ is accomplished in various ways. 의사소통

③ The sun went _____ a cloud. 뒤에

④ The _____ was his first job. 단체, 회사

⑤ We _____ that the earth is round. 믿다, ~라고 믿다

⑥ It is very unpleasant to _____ with him. 비유하다, 비교하다

⑦ The _____ rang to tell me the time. 종, 벨

⑧ Many people _____ about this product. 불평, 항의

⑨ English is my _____ subject. 최고, 제일 좋은

⑩ I want to _____ it. 완벽한, 완전한

> Communication company complete complain begin behind bell best compare believe

B 해석을 보고 빈칸에 해당되는 단어를 보기에서 찾아 적으세요.

① a _____ book 좋은[잘 쓴] 책
   Yes, that's a _____ point. 네, 그거 좋은 지적이십니다.

② ability to _____ 통치 능력
   _____ a church 교회를 관리하다.

③ an _____ box/glass 빈 상자/잔
   Is this an _____ chair? 이 의자 비었나요?

④ The _____ was driven back. 적은 격퇴되었다.
   the _____ of health 건강에 해로운 것

⑤ the _____ of the book 그 책의 말미
   There is no _____ to her talk. 그녀의 이야기는 한이 없다.

⑥ a diesel/petrol _____ 디젤/가솔린 엔진
   _____ trouble 엔진 고장

⑦ The money was _____. 돈을 다 써 버렸다.
   Is it _____ 3 yet? 벌써 3시 지났니?

> empty   end   gone   enemy   good   engine   govern

C 보기에 주어진 단어의 설명입니다. 해당되는 단어를 찾아 적으세요.

① 필요한 (유의어 essential)　　　　　　　　　　_____

② (동식물 등의) 자연　　　　　　　　　　　　　_____

③ 늦은, ~말의; 만년의 (반의어 early)　　　　　_____

④ ~ (at/about) (소리내어) 웃다　　　　　　　_____

⑤ (거리상으로) 가까운 (유의어 close)　　　　　_____

⑥ (앞장서서) 안내하다[이끌다/데리고 가다] (유의어 guide)　_____

⑦ (인위적으로 만든 것이 아닌) 자연[천연]의　　_____

| late | laugh | natural | nature | near | lead | necessary |

D 주어진 해석에 맞는 영어단어로 퍼즐을 완성하세요.

Across

1. 넓은, 너른
3. 시험
5. 인쇄하다
7. 회사, 단체
8. 불평하다
9. 믿다

Down

2. 빈, 비어있는
4. 어깨
6. 자연, 천성

A 주어진 문장에 맞는 단어를 보기에서 찾아 문장을 완성하세요.

❶ Do you have a _____ solution? 더 좋은

❷ The player is in the best _____. 상태

❸ He left _____ five and six o'clock. 사이에

❹ Please call me to _____. 확인

❺ I never eat a _____ dinner. 치수나 양 등이)큰

❻ I'm trying to _____ with you. 이어지다, 연결되다

❼ I bought a new mountain _____. 자전거

❽ There are too many things to _____ in this matter. 사려하다, 고려하다

❾ A _____ sits on the wire. 새

❿ The pockets _____ seeds. ~들어있다

> better confirm big bird contain consider connect condition between bike

B 해석을 보고 빈칸에 해당되는 단어를 보기에서 찾아 적으세요.

❶ Have you had _____? 배부르게[많이] 먹었니?

She sings well _____. 그 여자는 노래를 꽤 잘한다.

❷ an _____ contest 대등한 시합

_____ now it is not too late. 지금이라도 그리 늦지는 않다.

❸ _____ rights/pay 동등한 권리/급여

Ten times five is _____ to fifty. 10×5는 50

❹ Knock before you _____. 들어오기 전에 노크를 하시오.

to _____ data into a computer 컴퓨터에 자료를 입력하다

❺ a Yale _____ 예일대 졸업자

❻ a matter of _____ importance 대단히 중요한 문제

What a _____ goal! 정말 멋진 골이에요!

❼ a _____ design/plan/strategy 원대한 구상/계획/전략

a lot of _____ people 많은 저명인사들

> enough graduate enter grand equal even great

C 보기에 주어진 단어의 설명입니다. 해당되는 단어를 찾아 적으세요.

① (필수적이거나 아주 중요하므로) ~해야 하다 _____

② 배우다, 학습하다, ~을 알게 되다 _____

③ (사람, 장소에서) 떠나다, 출발하다 _____

④ 결코[절대/한 번도] ~않다 _____

⑤ 부정적인, 나쁜 (반의어 positive) _____

⑥ (크기규모가) 작은, 소규모의 _____

⑦ 왼쪽의, 좌측의 (반의어 right) _____

need	negative	left	little	learn	leave	never

D 주어진 해석에 맞는 영어단어로 퍼즐을 완성하세요.

Across

2. 확정하다
5. 적절한
6. 사이, 중간에
7. 동일시하다

Down

1. 생산물, 상품
2. 잇다, 연결하다
3. 은
4. 배우다, 학습하다
6. 자전거

801	**bit** [bit]	몡 조금, 약간	She's a bit of a mystery. 그녀는 약간 미스터리하다.
802	**continue** [kəntínjuː]	통 계속하다.	Even after the exam, you have to continue studying. 시험이 끝나도 계속해서 공부를 해야한다.
803	**evening** [íːvniŋ]	몡 저녁, 밤, 야간	I exercise every evening. 나는 저녁마다 운동을 한다.
804	**green** [griːn]	혱 녹색, 초록색	The leaves on the trees are turning green. 나무의 잎사귀들이 초록색으로 변하고 있다.
805	**length** [leŋkθ]	몡 길이, 기간	a journey of some length. 상당히 긴 여행
806	**new** [nuː]	혱 새, 새로운, 새 것	She was wearing a new coat. 그녀는 새로운 외투를 입고 있었다.
807	**pull** [pul]	통 끌다, 당기다	Pull the plug out. 플러그를 뽑아라.
808	**since** [sins]	젼 ~ 언제부터 졉 ~한 이후로, ~한 때로부터	She's been off work since Monday. 그녀는 월요일부터 휴가 중이다.
809	**there** [ðər]	뷔 거기에, 그곳에	Is there anybody there? 거기 아무도 없나요?
810	**wire** [waiər]	몡 전선, 철사	The machine works when the wire is connected. 기계은 전선이 연결되야 작동한다.

단어와 문장을 따라 쓰세요.

bit
She's a bit of a mystery.

continue
Even after the exam, you have to continue studying.

evening
I exercise every evening.

green
The leaves on the trees are turning green.

length
a journey of some length.

new
She was wearing a new coat.

pull
Pull the plug out.

since
She's been off work since Monday.

there
Is there anybody there?

wire
The machine works when the wire is connected.

811	**black** [blæk]	형 어두운, 캄캄한	He was all in black. 그는 전부 검은색 옷을 입고 있었다.
812	**control** [kəntróul]	명 지배, 통제	Children are hard to control. 아이들은 통제하기가 힘들다.
813	**event** [ivént]	명 행사	I prepared an event for her birthday. 나는 그녀의 생일을 위해 이벤트를 준비했다.
814	**grew** [gru:]	동 grow의 과거	I grew up a lot during the vacation. 나는 방학동안 많이 자랐다.
815	**less** [les]	부 더 적게, 덜하게	Its population is less than 1000. 그곳의 인구는 1000명이 안된다.
816	**next** [nekst]	형 다음	I get off at the next station. 나는 다음역에서 내려요.
817	**push** [puʃ]	동 밀다, 밀치다.	Push the door open. 밀면 문이 열린다.
818	**sing** [sɪŋ]	동 노래하다, 지저귀다, 울다	You can really sing! 노래를 정말 잘하는구나!
819	**these** [ðiːz]	형 이것	These toys are a real bargain. 이 장난감들은 정말 싸다.
820	**wish** [wiʃ]	동 원하다, 바라다.	I wish I were like you. 나는 너처럼 되고 싶다.

black

He was all in black.

control

Children are hard to control.

event

I prepared an event for her birthday.

grew

I grew up a lot during the vacation.

less

Its population is less than 1000.

next

I get off at the next station.

push

Push the door open.

sing

You can really sing!

these

These toys are a real bargain.

wish

I wish I were like you.

821	**block** [blak]	통 막다, 차단하다 명 관	It is important to block infectious diseases quickly. 전염병은 빨리 차단하는 것이 중요하다.
822	**conversation** [kɑ̀nvərséiʃən]	명 대화, 회화	I am taking English conversation classes. 나는 영어 회화 수업을 듣고 있다.
823	**ever** ['evə(r)]	부 (최상급의 의미), 언제나, 항상	It was raining harder than ever. 그 어느때보다 심하게 비가 내리고 있었다.
824	**ground** [graund]	명 땅바닥, 지면, 땅	The roots are below the ground. 뿌리는 땅 아래에 있다.
825	**lesson** [lésn]	명 수업, 가르침	There is a piano lesson after school. 방과후 피아노 레슨이 있다.
826	**night** [nait]	명 밤, 야간	I have nightmares every night. 나는 매일밤 악몽을 꾼다.
827	**put** [put]	통 (특정한 장소·위치에) 놓다 통 (사물, 사람) 밀어[집 어] 넣다	Put some oil in the car. 차에 기름을 좀 넣어주세요.
828	**single** [síŋgl]	형 단 하나의, 단일의	She wants to stay single forever. 그녀는 영원히 독신으로 살길 원한다.
829	**they** [ðeɪ]	대 그들, 그것들 대 (일반) 사람들	They arrived at 7.30 그들은 7시 30분에 도착했다.
830	**with** [wəð]	전 …와 함께 전 …로, …을 써서	I want a little talk with you. 당신과 함께 이야기하고 싶습니다.

단어와 문장을 따라 쓰세요.

block
It is important to block infectious diseases quickly.

conversation
I am taking English conversation classes.

ever
It was raining harder than ever.

ground
The roots are below the ground.

lesson
There is a piano lesson after school.

night
I have nightmares every night.

put
Put some oil in the car.

single
She wants to stay single forever.

they
They arrived at 7. 30

with
I want a little talk with you.

831	**blood** [blʌd]	뎽 피, 혈액	Blood donation is a life-saving thing. 헌혈은 생명을 구하는 것이다.
832	**cook** [kuk]	통 요리하다 뎽 요리사	Who will cook today? 오늘은 누가 요리할까?
833	**every** ['evri]	한 가능한 모든, 충분한	I go jogging every evening. 나는 저녁마다 조깅을 한다.
834	**group** [gruːp]	뎽 무리, 집단	He sings in a rock group. 그는 락 그룹에서 노래한다.
835	**let** [let]	통 ~하게 놓아두다, 허락 하다.	Please let me past. 저좀 지나가게 해주세요.
836	**noise** [nɔiz]	뎽 소리, 잡음	There's a lot of noise in the car when you drive. 운전할때 차에서 소음이 많이 발생한다.
837	**question** [kwéstʃən]	뎽 질문, 문제 통 질문하다, 심문하다, 설문 조사하다	Thank you, good question. 고맙습니다. 좋은 질문이군요.
838	**sister** [sístər]	뎽 언니, 누나, 여동생	I and my sister started working together. 나와 언니는 일을 같이 시작했다.
839	**thick** [θik]	혱 두꺼운, 두툼한	The thick paper doesn't fold well. 두꺼운 종이는 잘 접히지 않는다.
840	**woman** [wúmən]	뎽 여자, 성인여자	The woman was full of confidence. 그 여자는 자신감이 넘쳤다.

blood

Blood donation is a life-saving thing.

cook

Who will cook today?

every

I go jogging every evening.

group

He sings in a rock group.

let

Please let me past.

noise

There's a lot of noise in the car when you drive.

question

Thank you, good question.

sister

I and my sister started working together.

thick

The thick paper doesn't fold well.

woman

The woman was full of confidence.

841	**blue** [blu:]	형 파란, 푸른	We painted the wall deep blue. 우리는 벽을 짙은 파랑색으로 칠했다.
842	**cool** [ku:l]	형 시원한, 서늘한	I need cool water now. 나는 지금 시원한 물이 필요하다.
843	**exact** [ɪɡˈzækt]	형 꼼꼼한, 빈틈없는	I have the exact change. 저에게 잔돈이 맞게 있어요.
844	**grow** [grou]	동 잘하다, 커지다. 명 성장.	Where did you grow up? 당신은 어디서 자랐나요?
845	**letter** [létər]	명 편지, 글자, 문자	He handed me the letter. 그는 나에게 편지를 건넸다.
846	**noon** [nu:n]	명 정오, 낮 12시, 한낮	I have to go to Busan by noon. 나는 정오까지 부산에 가야한다.
847	**quick** [kwik]	부 빨리, 신속히 형 빠른	I prefer quick tempo music. 나는 빠른 박자의 음악을 좋아해.
848	**sit** [sɪt]	동 앉다, 앉아 있다	Can I sit next to you? 네 옆에 앉아도 되겠니?
849	**thin** [θɪn]	형 얇은, 가는	Thin books are not burdensome to read. 얇은 책은 읽기에 부담스럽지 않다.
850	**women** [wímin]	명 woman의 복수	The women were both Korean. 그 여자들은 둘 다 한국 사람이었다.

blue

We painted the wall deep blue.

cool

I need cool water now.

exact

I have the exact change.

grow

Where did you grow up?

letter

He handed me the letter.

noon

I have to go to Busan by noon.

quick

I prefer quick tempo music.

sit

Can I sit next to you?

thin

Thin books are not burdensome to read.

women

The women were both Korean.

851	**board** [bɔːrd]	명 판자, 널, 게시판	He's writing a story on the board. 남자가 게시판에 글을 쓰고 있다.
852	**copy** [kápi]	통 복사하다.	Could you make a copy of this document? 이 문서를 복사해 주시겠어요?
853	**example** [igzǽmpl]	명 예, 본보기,	Good example. Bad example. 좋은 예, 나쁜 예.
854	**guess** [ges]	통 추측하다, 알아맞히다.	Guess who I'm meeting? 내가 누굴 만났는지 알아 맞춰봐?
855	**level** [lévəl]	명 수준, 정도	The higher the score, the higher the level. 점수가 높을 수록 수준이 높다.
856	**normal** [nɔ́ːrməl]	형 보통의, 평범한, 정상적인	I want to live a normal life without hurting. 다치지 않고 평범한 삶을 살고싶다.
857	**quiet** [kwáiət]	형 조용한	They wanted to live in a quiet place. 그들은 조용한 곳에서 살고 싶었다.
858	**size** [saiz]	명 크기, 치수(표기)	What's your shoe size? 신발 사이즈가 어떻게 되요?
859	**thing** [θiŋ]	명 (생명이 없는) 사물, 것	I couldn't eat another thing. 나는 더 이상 먹을 수 없을 것 같다.
860	**wonder** [wʌndər]	통 궁금하다, ~일지 모르겠다.	I wonder who that letter was from. 나는 그 편지가 누구에게 온것인지 궁금하다.

board

He's writing a story on the board.

copy

Could you make a copy of this document?

example

Good example.   Bad example.

guess

Guess who I'm meeting?

level

The higher the score, the higher the level.

normal

I want to live a normal life without hurting.

quiet

They wanted to live in a quiet place.

size

What's your shoe size?

thing

I couldn't eat another thing.

wonder

I wonder who that letter was from.

861	**boat** [bout]	몡 배, 보트	The boat was sturdily made. 그 보트는 튼튼하게 만들어졌다.
862	**corn** [kɔːrn]	몡 옥수수, 곡식	Corn is a typical snack. 옥수수는 대표적인 간식이다.
863	**excellent** [ˈeksələnt]	혱 훌륭한, 탁월한	Her English pronunciation is excellent. 그녀의 영어발음은 훌륭하다.
864	**guest** [gest]	몡 손님, 투숙객	I was on the stage as a guest. 저는 게스트로 무대에 섰습니다.
865	**lie** [lai]	됭 누워 있다, 눕다 됭 거짓말하다,	I ordered the dog to lie down. 개에게 누우라고 명령했다.
866	**north** [nɔːrθ]	몡 북쪽, 북부	A compass needle points north. 나침반이 북쪽을 가리킨다.
867	**quite** [kwait]	븜 아주, 정말, 꽤, 상당히	They are quite good. 그들은 꽤 잘한다.
868	**skill** [skil]	몡 기술, 기량	He has a lack of skill at writing. 그는 글쓰는 기술이 부족하다.
869	**think** [θiŋk]	됭 생각하다, 사고하다.	I think you are fat. 나는 네가 뚱뚱하다고 생각해.
870	**wood** [wud]	몡 나무, 목재	All the furniture was made of wood. 모든 가구는 목재로 만들어져 있었다.

boat

The boat was sturdily made.

corn

Corn is a typical snack.

excellent

Her English pronunciation is excellent.

guest

I was on the stage as a guest.

lie

I ordered the dog to lie down.

north

A compass needle points north.

quite

They are quite good.

skill

He has a lack of skill at writing.

think

I think you are fat.

wood

All the furniture was made of wood.

871	**bone** [boun]	몡 뼈	The dog was chewing on a bone. 개는 뼈다귀를 물어 뜯고 있었다.
872	**corner** [kɔ́ːrnər]	몡 모서리, 모퉁이	If you turn the corner, you will see a bakery. 모퉁이를 돌면 빵집이 보인다.
873	**except** [iksépt]	젭 ~ 것만 제외하면, …라는 것 외에는 젠 ~ 제외하고는	We work every day except on weekends. 우리는 주말 외에는 매일 일한다.
874	**guide** [gaid]	몡 안내, 가이드 동 안내하여 보여주다	It is hard to travel without a guide. 가이드 없이는 여행하는 것이 힘듭니다.
875	**life** [laif]	몡 살아있음. 삶	She's had a hard life. 그녀는 힘든 삶을 살았다.
876	**nose** [nouz]	몡 코	My nose is stuffy because I have a cold. 감기가 걸려 코가 답답하다.
877	**race** [reis]	몡 경주, 달리기	The race is open to all. 그 경기는 누구라도 참가할 수 있다.
878	**skin** [skin]	몡 피부, 껍질	She wanted to have soft skin. 그녀는 부드러운 피부를 갖고 싶었다.
879	**third** [θəːrd]	서수 셋째의, 제3의	She finished in third place. 그녀는 3위로 들어왔다.
880	**word** [wəːrd]	몡 단어, 낱말 동 (특정한) 단어를 쓰다	She sent me word to come. 그녀는 나에게 오라는 단어를 보냈다.

bone
The dog was chewing on a bone.

corner
If you turn the corner, you will see a bakery.

except
We work every day except on weekends.

guide
It is hard to travel without a guide.

life
She's had a hard life.

nose
My nose is stuffy because I have a cold.

race
The race is open to all.

skin
She wanted to have soft skin.

third
She finished in third place.

word
She sent me word to come.

881	**book** [buk]	명 책 동 예약하다	I love this type of book. 나는 이런 종류의 책을 좋아한다.
882	**correct** [kərékt]	형 맞는, 적절한, 옳은	Your answer is correct. 네 답이 맞다.
883	**exchange** [ɪksˈtʃeɪndʒ]	명 교환, 주고받음, 맞바꿈	There are many exchange stations at the airport. 공항에는 많은 환전소가 있다.
884	**gun** [gʌn]	명 총, 대포	The gun must be handled with caution. 총은 조심히 다루어야 한다.
885	**lift** [lift]	동 들리다, 올라가다. 리프트	A lift is needed to move this thing. 이것들을 옮기려면 리프트가 필요하다.
886	**note** [nout]	명 메모, 쪽지	I put the note in my pocket. 나는 쪽지를 내 주머니에 넣었다.
887	**radio** [réidiòu]	명 라디오 동 무선연락을하다	I listen to the radio when I rest. 나는 휴식할때 라디오를 듣는다.
888	**sky** [skai]	명 하늘	My favorite color is sky-blue. 내가 좋아하는 색깔은 하늘 색이다.
889	**this** [ðis]	한, 대 이, 이것 부 이 정도로, 이렇게	Any plan this weekend? 이번 주말에 무슨 계획있니?
890	**work** [wəːrk]	동 일하다, 근무하다 명 일, 직장, 직업	I've finished my work. 난 일을 끝냈다.

단어와 문장을 따라 쓰세요.

book
I love this type of book.

correct
Your answer is correct.

exchange
There are many exchange stations at the airport.

gun
The gun must be handled with caution.

lift
A lift is needed to move this thing.

note
I put the note in my pocket.

radio
I listen to the radio when I rest.

sky
My favorite color is sky-blue.

this
Any plan this weekend?

work
I've finished my work.

891	**born** [bɔːrn]	통 태어나다. 생기다	He was born in the city but lived in the countryside. 그는 도시에서 태어났지만 시골에서 살았다.
892	**cost** [kɔːst]	명 값, 비용	The cost was charged too much. 비용이 너무 많이 청구되었다.
893	**excite** [iksáit]	통 흥분하다, 자극하다.	You excite his curiosity. 당신이 그의 호기심을 자극했다.
894	**hair** [hɛər]	명 머리, 머리카락	She had short curly hair. 그녀는 짧은 곱슬머리를 하고 있다.
895	**light** [lait]	명 빛, 광선, 밝음. 형 밝은	Wait for the light to turn green. 불이 초록색으로 바뀔때까지 기다려.
896	**nothing** [nʌθiŋ]	대 아무것도 아니다.	There was nothing in her bag. 그녀의 가방에는 아무것도 없었다.
897	**rain** [rein]	명 비, 빗물 통 비가오다	He walked in the rain. 그는 비를 맞으며 걸었다.
898	**slave** [sleiv]	명 노예	The boss treated me like a slave. 사장은 나를 노예처럼 취급했다.
899	**those** [ðouz]	형 그것들의 대 그들	Can I help you with those files? 그 파일들을 찾는거 도와 드릴까요?
900	**world** [wɜːrld]	명 세계	I'd like to travel around the world. 나는 세계 여행을 하고 싶다.

born

He was born in the city but lived in the countryside.

cost

The cost was charged too much.

excite

You excite his curiosity.

hair

She had short curly hair.

light

Wait for the light to turn green.

nothing

There was nothing in her bag.

rain

He walked in the rain.

slave

The boss treated me like a slave.

those

Can I help you with those files?

world

I'd like to travel around the world.

A 주어진 문장에 맞는 단어를 보기에서 찾아 문장을 완성하세요.

❶ She's a _____ of a mystery. 조금, 약간

❷ Even after the exam, you have to _____ studying. 계속하다

❸ He was all in _____. 검은색

❹ Children are hard to _____. 지배, 통제

❺ It is important to _____ infectious diseases quickly. 막다, 차단하다

❻ I am taking English _____ classes. 대화, 회화

❼ _____ donation is a life-saving thing. 피, 혈액

❽ Who will _____ today? 요리하다

❾ We painted the wall deep _____. 파란, 푸른

❿ I need _____ water now. 시원한, 서늘한

continue blood conversation control bit cool cook block black blue

B 해석을 보고 빈칸에 해당되는 단어를 보기에서 찾아 적으세요.

❶ to _____ bigger/taller 몸집/키가 더 커지다

　 to _____ old/bored/calm 나이를 먹다/지루해지다/잠잠해지다

❷ the _____-growing problem 자꾸 커지는 문제

　 She is _____ the same. 그녀는 예나 다름없다

❸ What were his _____ words? 그가 정확히 무슨 말을 했나?

　 an _____ description 정확한 묘사

❹ a main _____ 주요한 시합[경기]

　 an annual _____ 연중행사

❺ a _____ of girls / trees / houses 한 무리의 소녀/나무/집

　 a _____ activity 집단 활동

❻ _____ fields/hills 초록빛 들판/산들

　 _____ movements 환경 보호 운동

❼ an older/younger _____ 언니[누나]/여동생[(어린) 누이]

　 She's my _____. 그녀는 제 언니[누나/여동생]예요.

green   event   ever   group   exact   grow   sister

C 보기에 주어진 단어의 설명입니다. 해당되는 단어를 찾아 적으세요.

❶ 수업[교습/교육] (시간) (참조 class) _____

❷ 더 적은[덜한]; 더 적은[덜한] 것 _____

❸ 그 다음[뒤]에, 그리고는 _____

❹ 정오, 낮 12시, 한낮 (유의어 midday) _____

❺ 새, 새로운 (반의어 old) _____

❻ (듣기 싫은·시끄러운) 소리, 소음 _____

❼ 글자, 문자, 편지 _____

| new | less | next | lesson | noise | letter | noon |

D 주어진 해석에 맞는 영어단어로 퍼즐을 완성하세요.

Across

2. 피, 혈액
4. 지배, 통제
5. 녹색, 초록색
6. 요리하다
7. 원하다, 바라다
8. 끌다, 당기다

Down

1. 땅바닥, 지면
3. 검정, 어두운
4. 계속하다

A 주어진 문장에 맞는 단어를 보기에서 찾아 문장을 완성하세요.

❶ He's writing a story on the _____. 판자, ~판

❷ Could you make a _____ of this document? 복사

❸ The _____ was sturdily made. 배

❹ _____ is a typical snack. 옥수수

❺ The dog was chewing on a _____. 뼈

❻ If you turn the _____, you will see a bakery. 모서리, 모퉁이

❼ I love this type of _____. 책

❽ Your answer is _____. 적절한, 옳은

❾ He was _____ in the city but lived in the countryside. 태어나다

❿ The _____ was charged too much. 값, 비용

> cost   correct   bone   boat   born   copy   book   corner   corn   board

B 해석을 보고 빈칸에 해당되는 단어를 보기에서 찾아 적으세요.

❶ Everyone is ready _____ you. 너 말고는 다 준비되어 있다.

_____ by agreement 협정에 의한 것을 제외하고는

❷ _____ a thing 물건을 바꾸다

_____ greetings 인사를 주고받다

❸ an _____ meal 훌륭한 식사

She speaks _____ French. 그녀는 뛰어난 프랑스어를 구사한다.

❹ a _____ to Family Health 가족 건강 안내서

a tour _____ 관광 가이드

❺ give an _____ 예를 들다

for _____ 예를 들면

❻ Can you _____ his age? 그의 나이를 추측해 볼 수 있겠니?

_____ the woman's age at 25 그 여자의 나이를 25살로 추측하다

❼ Don't _____ yourself. 흥분하지 마.

_____ a person to anger 남을 화나게 하다

> example   guess   excellent   except   guide   exchange   excite

C 보기에 주어진 단어의 설명입니다. 해당되는 단어를 찾아 적으세요.

❶ (격식을 차리지 않은 짧은) 편지, 쪽지 _____

❷ (가치·질 등의) 수준[단계] _____

❸ 살아 있음, 삶, 생(명) _____

❹ 보통의, 평범한, 정상적인 _____

❺ (위로) 들어 올리다[올리다]; 들리다, 올라가다 _____

❻ 빛, (날이) 밝은, (빛이) 밝은 [환한] _____

❼ 아무것도[단 하나도] (~아니다·없다) _____

| level | normal | life | lift | note | light | nothing |

D 주어진 해석에 맞는 영어단어로 퍼즐을 완성하세요.

Across

2. 생각하다
3. 모서리, 모퉁이
4. 안내, 가이드
6. 보통의, 평범한
8. 훌륭한, 탁월한

Down

1. 사물, 것
3. 맞는, 옳은
5. 예, 본보기
7. 손님, 투숙객

901	**both** [bouθ]	한, 대 둘 다, ~뿐만 아니라, ~도	I liked them both. 나는 그들이 둘다 좋았다.
902	**cotton** [kátn]	명 목화, 면	These clothes are 100% cotton. 이 옷들은 100% 순면이다.
903	**exercise** [éksərsàiz]	명 운동 동 행동하다.	Walking is good exercise. 걷는 건 좋은 운동이다.
904	**half** [hæf]	명 반, 절반, 전반의	The glass was half full. 유리잔은 절반쯤 차 있었다.
905	**like** [laik]	전 ~와 같은, 비슷한 동 ~을 좋아하다.	I like spicy food. 나는 매운 음식을 좋아해.
906	**notice** [nóutis]	명 신경씀, 주목, 알아챔 명 공고문	I didn't notice him leaving. 나는 그가 떠나는 것을 알지 못했다.
907	**raise** [reiz]	동 들어올리다, 일으키다.	She got a salary raise. 그녀는 월급이 올랐다.
908	**sleep** [sliːp]	동 자다.	I need to get some sleep. 나는 잠을 좀 자야 한다.
909	**though** [ðou]	접 ~이긴 하지만, ~이기는 하다. 부 그렇지만	I tried my best, though. 하지만, 난 최선을 다했다.
910	**would** [wəd]	조 ~일[할] 것이다	Would you have dinner with me on Friday? 금요일 저와함께 저녁 식사 같이 하실래요?

단어와 문장을 따라 쓰세요.

both
I liked them both.

cotton
These clothes are 100% cotton.

exercise
Walking is good exercise.

half
The glass was half full.

like
I like spicy food.

notice
I didn't notice him leaving.

raise
She got a salary raise.

sleep
I need to get some sleep.

though
I tried my best, though.

would
Would you have dinner with me on Friday?

911	**bottle** [bátl]	몡 병	He was selling juice in a bottle. 그는 병에 든 주스를 팔고 있었다.
912	**could** [kəd]	조 can의 과거형	Could you drive me home? 나를 집까지 태워다 줄 수 있겠니?
913	**expect** [ikspékt]	통 예상하다. 기대하다.	Do you expect him to come early? 그가 일찍 올 거라고 예상하나요?
914	**hand** [hænd]	몡 손, ~손을 사용하는 통 건네주다, 넘겨주다	The dog's bite hurt my hand. 강아지가 손을 물어서 아팠다.
915	**limited** [límitid]	혱 제한된, 한정된	Only limited products are sold. 한정된 제품만 판매합니다.
916	**noun** [naun]	몡 (문법) 명사	An adjective or a noun? 형용사 아니면 명사?
917	**ran** [ræn]	몡 run의 과거	He ran out the door. 그가 문밖으로 달려 나갔다.
918	**slip** [slip]	통 미끄러지다. 몡 실수	Mind! You'll slip. 조심해! 미끄러집니다.
919	**thought** [θɔːt]	몡 생각, 사고력	I thought the play was rubbish! 내 생각에 그 연극은 쓰레기였다!
920	**write** [rait]	통 쓰다, 집필하다, 작성하다	Can he read and write? 글을 읽고 쓸 줄 아나요?

bottle

He was selling juice in a bottle.

could

Could you drive me home?

expect

Do you expect him to come early?

hand

The dog's bite hurt my hand.

limited

Only limited products are sold.

noun

An adjective or a noun?

ran

He ran out the door.

slip

Mind! You'll slip.

thought

I thought the play was rubbish!

write

Can he read and write?

921	**bottom** [bátəm]	몡 맨 아래, 뒷면	There is a hole in the bottom of the stomach. 배 밑바닥에 구멍이 생겼다.
922	**count** [kaunt]	동 세다, 계산하다.	Count from one to ten. 1에서 10까지 세다.
923	**expensive** [ikspénsiv]	혱 비싼, 돈이 많이 드는	Musical tickets are too expensive. 뮤지컬 티켓은 너무 비싸다.
924	**happen** [hǽpən]	동 있다, ~ 일어나다.	It can happen. 그럴 수 있다.
925	**line** [lain]	몡 줄, 선	Don't erase the line. 그 선을 지우지 마시오.
926	**novel** [návəl]	몡 소설 혱 새로운 신기함	This novel is too boring. 이 소설은 너무 지루하다.
927	**range** [reindʒ]	몡 다양성, 범위	This missile range is very long. 이 미사일 사정 거리는 매우 길다.
928	**slow** [slou]	혱 느린, 더딘, 천천히 움직이는	The postal service is too slow. 우체국 서비스가 너무 느리다.
929	**thousand** [θáuzənd]	쉬 천, 1,000	A thousand people were there. 그곳에는 천명의 사람들이 있었다.
930	**written** [rítn]	혱 글로 표현 된, 필기로 된	The written letter remains. 쓰여진 편지는 남는다.

  단어와 문장을 따라 쓰세요.

bottom
There is a hole in the bottom of the stomach.

count
Count from one to ten.

expensive
Musical tickets are too expensive.

happen
It can happen.

line
Don't erase the line.

novel
This novel is too boring.

range
This missile range is very long.

slow
The postal service is too slow.

thousand
A thousand people were there.

written
The written letter remains.

931	**bought** [bɔːt]	동 buy의 과거, 과거분사	I think I bought it too much. 내가 그것을 너무 많이 산거 같다.
932	**country** [kʌntri]	명 국가, 나라	The country is now at war. 그 나라는 지금 전쟁중이다.
933	**experience** [ikspíəriəns]	명 경험 동 경험하다	I learn a lot from experience. 경험을 통해 많은 것을 배운다.
934	**happy** [hǽpi]	형 행복한	You look so happy. 대단히 행복해 보인다.
935	**link** [liŋk]	동 연결하다.	Anybody can paste in a link. 누구나 링크를 가져 갈 수 있다.
936	**now** [nau]	부 지금, 이제	I saw her just now. 나는 방금전에 그녀를 봤다.
937	**reach** [riːtʃ]	동 이르다, 도달하다.	What conclusions did you reach? 어떤 결론에 도달했나요?
938	**small** [smɔːl]	형 (크기,수,양) 작은[적은], 소규모의 부 잘게	That dress is too small for you. 그 드레스는 너에게 너무 작다.
939	**through** [θruː]	전 ~을 통해 ~사이로 부 ~지나, ~사이로	She went through that door. 그 여자는 저 문으로 들어갔다.
940	**wrong** [rɔ́ːŋ]	형 틀린, 잘못된	The wrong thing must be corrected quickly. 잘못된 것은 빨리 고쳐야 한다.

bought

I think I bought it too much.

country

The country is now at war.

experience

I learn a lot from experience.

happy

You look so happy.

link

Anybody can paste in a link.

now

I saw her just now.

reach

What conclusions did you reach?

small

That dress is too small for you.

through

She went through that door.

wrong

The wrong thing must be corrected quickly.

941	**bowl** [boul]	몡 그릇, 통	We each ate a bowl of rice. 우리는 각자 밥 한 그릇씩 먹었다.
942	**course** [kɔːrs]	몡 강의, 강좌, 과정	How long is the course? 그 과정은 얼마나 걸리나요?
943	**experiment** [ikspérəmənt]	몡 실험 동 실험을 하다	This experiment has a time limit. 이 실험은 시간 제약이 있다.
944	**hard** [haːrd]	형 단단한, 굳은, 어려운 부 열심히	She's had a hard life. 그녀는 어려운 생활을 해왔다.
945	**list** [list]	몡 목록, 명단	Is your name on the list? 너의 이름이 명단에 있니?
946	**number** [nʌmbər]	몡 수, 숫자 동 순서를 매기다.	What is your phone number? 너의 전화번호가 뭐니?
947	**read** [riːd]	동 읽다, 읽어 주다 몡 읽기, 독서	She read us a story. 그녀가 우리에게 이야기를 읽어주었다.
948	**smell** [smel]	동 냄새가 나다	I smell good at home. 집에서 좋은 냄새가 난다.
949	**throw** [θrou]	동 던지다, 내던지다.	When I got home, I threw my bag away. 집에 오자마자 가방을 내 던졌다.
950	**wrote** [rout]	동 write의 과거	She wrote a biography of Beethoven. 그녀는 베토벤의 전기를 썼다.

단어와 문장을 따라 쓰세요.

bowl

We each ate a bowl of rice.

course

How long is the course?

experiment

This experiment has a time limit.

hard

She's had a hard life.

list

Is your name on the list?

number

What is your phone number?

read

She read us a story.

smell

I smell good at home.

throw

When I got home, I threw my bag away.

wrote

She wrote a biography of Beethoven.

951	**box** [baks]	명 상자, 갑	How heavy is the box? 그 상자는 무게가 얼마나 될까요?
952	**cover** [kʌvər]	동 덮다. 씌우다. 명 덮개	Cover her over with a blanket. 그녀에게 담요를 덮어 주어라.
953	**express** [iksprés]	형 급행의, 신속한	Please send this letter to express. 이 편지는 속달로 보내주세요.
954	**has** [həz]	동 have의 제3인칭	She has a lovely voice. 그녀는 사랑스런 목소리를 가졌다.
955	**listen** [lísn]	동 듣다, 귀 기울이다.	Listen to me! 내말 들어봐!
956	**numeral** [njú:mərəl]	명 숫자, 수사	Arabic numeral. 아라비아 숫자.
957	**ready** [rédi]	형 준비가 된 동 준비시키다.	Dinner is ready out. 저녁 준비가 다 되었다.
958	**smile** [smaɪl]	동 웃다, 미소 짓다	She gave a thin smile. 그녀가 희미한 미소를 지어 보였다.
959	**tie** [tai]	동 묶다, 달다 명 넥타이	Please tie the paper box together. 종이 상자를 함께 묶어 주세요.
960	**yard** [jɑːrd]	명 마당, 뜰	Pretty flowers bloomed in the yard. 마당에 이쁜 꽃들이 피었다.

box
How heavy is the box?

cover
Cover her over with a blanket.

express
Please send this letter to express.

has
She has a lovely voice.

listen
Listen to me!

numeral
Arabic numeral.

ready
Dinner is ready out.

smile
She gave a thin smile.

tie
Please tie the paper box together.

yard
Pretty flowers bloomed in the yard.

961	**boy** [bɔi]	명 소년, 남자아이	I used to play here as a boy. 내가 어렸을때 이곳에서 놀곤했다.
962	**cow** [kau]	명 암소, 젖소	He's leading the cow. 그는 소를 끌고가고 있다.
963	**extra** [ékstrə]	명 추가되는 것	The extra charge came out due to the weight excess. 중량 초과로 추가 요금이 나왔다.
964	**hat** [hæt]	명 모자, 직책	It is good to wear a hat on a cold day. 추운 날에는 모자를 쓰는 것이 좋다.
965	**little** [lítl]	형 작은, 소규모의 한, 대 거의 없는	I play the piano a little. 나는 피아노를 조금 친다.
966	**nurse** [nəːrs]	명 간호사	I'd like to be a nurse. 간호사가 되고 싶다.
967	**real** [ríːəl]	형 진짜, 실제 부 정말, 아주	The maths exam was a real beast. 수학 시험은 정말 끔찍했다.
968	**snow** [snou]	명 눈 동 눈이오다	It was beginning to snow. 눈이 오기 시작하고 있었다.
969	**time** [taɪm]	명 시간, 시기나 때를 맞추다.	Time changes everything. 시간은 모든 것을 바꾼다.
970	**year** [jiər]	명 1년[한 해]	Spring came late this year. 올해는 봄이 늦게 왔다.

boy

I used to play here as a boy.

cow

He's leading the cow.

extra

The extra charge came out due to the weight excess.

hat

It is good to wear a hat on a cold day.

little

I play the piano a little.

nurse

I'd like to be a nurse.

real

The maths exam was a real beast.

snow

It was beginning to snow.

time

Time changes everything.

year

Spring came late this year.

971	**brain** [brein]	명 뇌	I did a brain test in a traffic accident. 교통 사고로 뇌 검사를 했다.
972	**creative** [kriéitiv]	형 창조적인, 창의적인	I am preparing for a creative class. 창의적인 수업을 준비하고 있다.
973	**eye** [ai]	명 눈 동 쳐다보다	I have something in my eye. 내 눈에 뭐가 들어갔다.
974	**hate** [heit]	동 미워하는, 싫어하는	I hate Sunday evening. 나는 일요일 저녁이 싫다.
975	**live** [liv]	동 살다 형 살아 있는, 생방송의	Do you live near here? 가까운 곳에서 살고 계신가요?
976	**object** [ábdʒikt]	명 물건, 물체 동 반대하다	The object was huge. 그 물체는 거대했다.
977	**reason** [ríːzn]	명 이유, 까닭, 사유	Tell me the real reason. 진짜 이유를 말해봐.
978	**so** [sou]	부 정말(로), 너무나, 대단히 접 그래서	So, tell me more. 그래서, 더 이야기 해봐
979	**tiny** [táini]	형 아주 작은	There was a tiny hole in the window. 창문에 아주 작은 구멍이 생겼다.
980	**yellow** [jélou]	형 노란, 노란색의	It is better to stop at yellow signals. 노란색 신호에는 멈추는 것이 좋다.

brain

I did a brain test in a traffic accident.

creative

I am preparing for a creative class.

eye

I have something in my eye.

hate

I hate Sunday evening.

live

Do you live near here?

object

The object was huge.

reason

Tell me the real reason.

so

So, tell me more.

tiny

There was a tiny hole in the window.

yellow

It is better to stop at yellow signals.

981	**branch** [bræntʃ]	몡 나뭇가지, 지사,지점	Unfortunately, each franchise branch has a different taste. 아쉽지만 프랜차이즈 지점마다 맛이 다르다.
982	**crop** [krap]	몡 작물, 수확량	Corn is an important crop on the island. 옥수수는 그 섬에 중요한 농작물이다.
983	**face** [feis]	몡 얼굴 동 마주보다	I never forget a face. 나는 사람들 얼굴을 절대 잊지 않는다.
984	**have** [həv]	동 가지다, 소유하다 동 …으로 되어있다	I have an important meeting on Monday. 나는 월요일에 중요한 미팅이 있다.
985	**loan** [loun]	몡 대출, 빌려 줌.	There are many loan products in the bank. 은행에는 많은 대출 상품이 있다.
986	**observe** [əbzɔ́:rv]	동 ~보다, 알다/목격하다	observe the change of nature. 자연의 변화를 관찰하다.
987	**receive** [risí:v]	동 받다, 받아들이다	Did you receive the fax? 팩스 받았나요?
988	**soft** [sɔ:ft]	형 부드러운, 푹신한	Her voice was soft and beautiful. 그녀의 목소리는 부드럽고 아름다웠다.
989	**tired** [taiər]	동 피곤해지다. 몡 타이어	She became tired from a long journey. 긴 여행으로 그녀는 피곤해있었다.
990	**yet** [jet]	뭐 아직	I didn't get my order yet. 주문한 음식이 아직 안 나왔습니다.

branch

Unfortunately, each franchise branch has a different taste.

crop

Corn is an important crop on the island.

face

I never forget a face.

have

I have an important meeting on Monday.

loan

There are many loan products in the bank.

observe

observe the change of nature.

receive

Did you receive the fax?

soft

Her voice was soft and beautiful.

tired

She became tired from a long journey.

yet

I didn't get my order yet.

991	**bread** [bred]	몡 빵	I ate bread and soup for breakfast. 아침으로 빵과 수프를 먹었습니다.
992	**cross** [krɔːs]	몡 십자가 X표 동 가로지르다	I hope I never cross her path again. 나는 그녀와 다시는 마추치지 않기 바란다.
993	**fact** [fækt]	몡 사실, 실제, 실상	The story is based on fact. 그 이야기는 사실에 기반을 두고 있다.
994	**he** [hi]	대 그, 그분	He acted like a gentleman. 그는 신사처럼 행동했다.
995	**locate** [lóukeit]	동 ~위치를 찾아내다. 사업을 시작하다	I must locate your son. 너의 아들의 위치를 찾아야한다.
996	**occur** [əkɔ́ːr]	동 일어나다, 발생하다	Crimes occur a lot at night. 범죄는 밤에 많이 발생한다.
997	**record** [rikɔ́ːrd]	동 기록하다 몡 기록, 레코드	He has smashed the world record. 그는 세계기록을 갈아 치웠다.
998	**soil** [sɔil]	몡 토양, 흙, 국가, 국토	Plants grow well in good soil. 좋은 흙에서 식물이 잘 자란다.
999	**together** [təgéðər]	뷔 함께, ~ 같이.	We always go everywhere together. 우리는 항상 함께 다닌다.
1000	**young** [jʌŋ]	혱 젊은, 어린	She looks young for her age. 그녀는 나이에 비해 젊어보인다.

bread
I ate bread and soup for breakfast.

cross
I hope I never cross her path again.

fact
The story is based on fact.

he
He acted like a gentleman.

locate
I must locate your son.

occur
Crimes occur a lot at night.

record
He has smashed the world record.

soil
Plants grow well in good soil.

together
We always go everywhere together.

young
She looks young for her age.

A 주어진 문장에 맞는 단어를 보기에서 찾아 문장을 완성하세요.

❶ I liked them _____ . 둘 다

❷ These clothes are 100% _____ . 목화, 면

❸ He was selling juice in a _____ . 병, 병에 담다

❹ _____ you drive me home? 무엇을 해 달라고 부탁할 때

❺ There is a hole in the _____ of the stomach. 맨 아래

❻ _____ from one to ten. 세다, 계산하다

❼ I think I _____ it too much. 사다, 구입하다

❽ We each ate a _____ of rice. 그릇, 통

❾ How long is the _____ ? 강의, 강좌, 코스

❿ The _____ is now at war. 나라, 국가

> cotton bought count could both country bowl bottom bottle course

B 해석을 보고 빈칸에 해당되는 단어를 보기에서 찾아 적으세요.

❶ learn by _____ 경험에 의하여 배우다

gain one's _____ 경험을 쌓다

❷ I shall _____ you. 기다리고 있겠습니다.

I _____ to do it. 그것을 할 작정이다.

❸ Swimming is good _____ . 수영은 좋은 운동이다.

_____ for the piano 피아노 연습

❹ Accidents will _____ . 사고는 일어나게 마련이다.

Something is likely to _____ 무슨 일이 일어날 것만 같다.

❺ Can you _____ me that towel? 그 수건 좀 내게 던져 주겠니?

_____ a bone to a dog 개에게 뼈를 던져 주다

❻ a _____ smile/face 행복한 미소/얼굴

The story has a _____ ending. 그 이야기는 행복하게 끝난다.

❼ _____ the fruit was bad. 그 과일은 절반이 썩어 있었다.

at _____ past ten 10시 반에

> exercise   half   expect   happen   experience   happy   throw

C 보기에 주어진 단어의 설명입니다. 해당되는 단어를 찾아 적으세요.

❶ (공공장소에 붙이는) 공고문[안내문], ~을 의식하다[(보거나 듣고) 알다] ＿＿＿＿＿＿＿

❷ ~와 비슷한, ~와 (똑)같이[마찬가지로], ~처럼 ＿＿＿＿＿＿＿

❸ 수, 숫자, 수사, (전화팩스 등의) 번호 ＿＿＿＿＿＿＿

❹ 제한된, 아주 많지는 않은, (시간·수 등이) 한정된 ＿＿＿＿＿＿＿

❺ 목록, 명단, (항목숫자들을 적어 놓은) 일람표 ＿＿＿＿＿＿＿

❻ (사람사물 사이의) 관련, (교통통신) 연결, 고리 ＿＿＿＿＿＿＿

❼ 지금, 이제, 당장에, 즉시 ＿＿＿＿＿＿＿

| like | notice | limited | link | now | list | number |

D 주어진 해석에 맞는 영어단어로 퍼즐을 완성하세요.

Across

3. 맨 아래
4. 운동
7. 소설
9. 행복한

Down

1. 쓰다, 집필하다
2. 제한된, 한정된
5. 국가, 나라
6. 절반
8. 작은, 소규모의

Review TEST 2

A 주어진 문장에 맞는 단어를 보기에서 찾아 문장을 완성하세요.

❶ How heavy is the _____ ? 상자, 갑

❷ _____ her over with a blanket. 덮다, 씌우다

❸ I used to play here as a _____ . 소년, 남자아이

❹ He's leading the _____ . 암소, 젖소

❺ I did a _____ test in a traffic accident. 뇌

❻ I am preparing for a _____ class. 창조, 창의

❼ Unfortunately, each franchise _____ has a different taste. 지사, 분점

❽ Corn is an important _____ on the island. 작물

❾ I ate _____ and soup for breakfast. 빵

❿ I hope I never _____ her path again. 교차하다

> cross   crop   brain   boy   bread   cover   branch   creative   cow   box

B 해석을 보고 빈칸에 해당되는 단어를 보기에서 찾아 적으세요.

❶ _____ you got a job yet? 당신은 이미 직장이 있습니까?

  _____ a letter to write 써야 할 편지가 있다

❷ an _____ bus/coach/train 급행 버스/(장거리) 버스/열차

  _____ mail 속달 우편

❸ a pretty/round/freckled _____ 예쁜/동그란/주근깨가 있는 얼굴

  a sad/happy/smiling _____ 슬픈/행복한/웃는 얼굴(표정)

❹ I _____ spinach. 난 시금치는 질색이야.

  I _____ Monday mornings. 난 월요일 아침이 너무 싫다.

❺ to charge/pay/cost _____ 추가로 부과하다/지불하다/비용이 들다

  an _____ inning game (야구의) 연장전

❻ to put on/take off a _____ 모자를 쓰다/벗다

  I take my _____ off to somebody ~께 경의를 표합니다.

❼ _____ went through that door. 그 남자는 저 문으로 들어갔다.

  Is your cat a _____ or a she? 댁의 고양이는 수컷입니까, 암컷입니까?

> express   extra   hat   hate   face   have   he

C 보기에 주어진 단어의 설명입니다. 해당되는 단어를 찾아 적으세요.

❶ <일이> 일어나다, 생기다, 발생하다, 떠오르다 _____

❷ <관찰> 알다, 보다, 목격하다, 주시하다 _____

❸ <크기규모가> 작은, 소규모의, <거리시간이> 짧은, 조금, 잠깐 _____

❹ <특정 위치에> 두다, ~의 정확한 위치를 찾아내다 _____

❺ <동작·감정·사상 등의> 대상, 물건, 물체 _____

❻ 준비가 된, 채비를 갖춘, 막 ~하려고 하는, 금방이라도 ~할 것 같은 _____

❼ 간호사, 간호하다, 병구완하다 _____

> ready   little   nurse   object   observe   locate   occur

D 주어진 해석에 맞는 영어단어로 퍼즐을 완성하세요.

Across

4. 간호사
6. 덮다, 씌우다
8. 창조적인
10. 나뭇가지, 지점

Down

1. 얼굴
2. 추가되는 것
3. 물건, 물체
5. 받다, 받아들이다
7. 이유, 사유
9. 급행의, 신속한

정 답

Review TEST Day 001 ~ Day 005

• Review TEST 1

A.
1. break   2. location
3. bridge   4. solution
5. famous   6. remember
7. cycle   8. some
9. dad   10. tool

B.
1. look   2. cut
3. famous   4. repeat
5. ocean   6. office
7. red

C.
1. solution   2. too
3. some   4. tool
5. soldier   6. tone
7. tell

D.

• Review TEST 2

A.
1. brought   2. accident
3. active   4. burn
5. build   6. brother
7. brown   8. act
9. actor   10. add

B.
1. damage   2. dark
3. fat   4. father
5. danger   6. fastest
7. dance

C.
1. low   2. help
3. love   4. loud
5. lot   6. here
7. heavy

D.

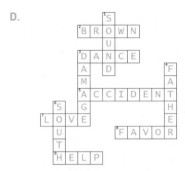

Review TEST Day 006 ~ Day 010

• Review TEST 1

A.
1. advantage   2. busy
3. advice   4. but
5. afraid   6. buy
7. after   8. by
9. again   10. cable

B.
1. decide   2. .fall
3. fell   4 . dear
5. dead   6. feed
7. his

C.
1. make   2. machine
3. main   4. magnet
5. history   6. lucky
7. high

D.

• Review TEST 2

A.
1. against   2. call
3. age   4. came
5. ago   6. camp
7. agree   8. campus
9. air   10. can

B.
1. few   2. design
3. fight   4. field

5. desert   6. depend

7. deep

C.   1. hold   2. manner

3. make   4. hit

5. holiday   6. hole

7. major

D.

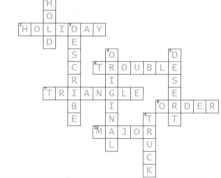

Review TEST Day 011 ~ Day 015

• **Review TEST 1**

A.   1. airline   2. capital

3. airport   4. captain

5. album   6. car

7. alive   8. card

9. all   10. care

B.   1. find   2. differ

3. dictionary   4. final

5. finger   6. desk

7. finish

C.   1. hope   2. market

3. mark   4. master

5. hot   6. mass

7. house

D.

• **Review TEST 2**

A.   1. allow   2. careful

3. also   4. carry

5. always   6. case

7. among   8. cat

9. anger   10. catch

B.   1. direct   2. difficult

3. fire   4. first

5. fish   6. fishing

7. dish

C.   1. material   2. may

3. human   4. huge

5. hunt   6. matter

7. match

D.

Review TEST Day 016 ~ Day 020

• **Review TEST 1**

A.   1. animal   2. caught

3. answer   4. cause

5. any   6. cell phone

7. anybody   8. center

9. appear   10. century

B.   1. divide   2. display

3. floor   4. flat

5. distant   6. fly

7. flower

C.   1. mean   2. hurt

3. idea   4. meet

5. hurry   6. melody

7. meat

D.

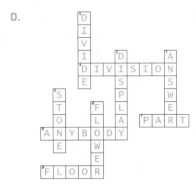

• Review TEST 2

A.
1. apple 2. certain
3. application 4. chair
5. area 6. chance
7. arm 8. change
9. army 10. character

B.
1. follow 2. include
3. document 4. foot
5. force 6. doctor
7. food

C.
1. include 2. imagine
3. independent 4. impossible
5. middle 6. may
7. mile

D.

P
A
   S   Y
   C   M
V I L L A G E
   I M A G I N E   T
   E
   S T R A N G E
   C
 C   C H A N G E
 H   O
 A   O
M I D D L E
 R

Review TEST Day 021 ~ Day 025

• Review TEST 1

A.
1. arrange 2. charge
3. arrive 4. chart
5. art 6. checkin
7. as 8. cheese

---

9. aside 10. chick

B.
1. draw 2. forward
3. form 4. fraction
5. forest 6. double
7. down

C.
1. indicate 2. million
3. mind 4. industry
5. instant 6. insurance
7. minister

D.

• Review TEST 2

A.
1. ask 2. child
3. at 4. childhood
5. atom 6. children
7. average 8. choose
9. baby 10. circle

B.
1. drop 2. drink
3. free 4. freedom
5. dream 6. fresh
7. dress

C.
1. modern 2. iron
3. invent 4. mistake
5. mix 6. job
7. miss

D.

            D
         M R
       C I R C L E
         I A
   P   S M
   I S T
 P I C T U R E S
   E C A U
   A V E R A G E
      S E N
  F R E S H

Review TEST Day 026 ~ Day 030

• Review TEST 1

A.
1. back
2. city
3. bad
4. claim
5. balance
6. class
7. ball
8. classroom
9. band
10. clean

B.
1. during
2. each
3. fruit
4. dry
5. front
6. full
7. game

C.
1. join
2. moment
3. month
4. joy
5. jump
6. journalist
7. more

D.

• Review TEST 2

A.
1. bank
2. clear
3. bars
4. client
5. base
6. climb
7. basis
8. clock
9. basketball
10. close

B.
1. early
2. gather
3. Earth
4. garden
5. gas
6. east
7. ear

C.
1. keep
2. most
3. motion
4. just
5. mount
6. morning
7. kill

D.

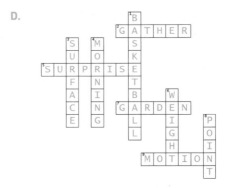

Review TEST Day 031 ~ Day 035

• Review TEST 1

A.
1. bat
2. clothe
3. beach
4. cloud
5. bear
6. post
7. beat
8. beauty
9. cold
10. power

B.
1. edge
2. eat
3. gentle
4. editor
5. gift
6. egg

C.
1. know
2. move
3. much
4. kind
5. lady
6. multiply
7. power

D.

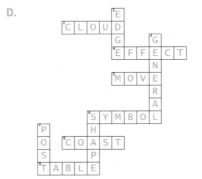

• Review TEST 2

A.
1. bed
2. collect
3. bedroom
4. colony
5. been
6. color
7. before
8. come
9. began
10. common

B.
1. either
2. give

3. go   4. global
5. glass   6. electric
7. glad

C.   1. land   2. language
3. large   4. name
5. museum   6. must
7. music

D.

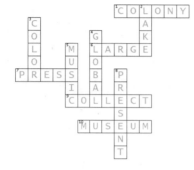

Review TEST Day 036 ~ Day 040

• **Review TEST 1**

A.   1. begin   2. communication
3. behind   4. company
5. believe   6. compare
7. bell   8. complain
9. best   10. complete

B.   1. good   2. govern
3. empty   4. enemy
5. end   6. engine
7. gone

C.   1. necessary   2. nature
3. late   4. laugh
5. near   6. lead
7. natural

D.

• **Review TEST 2**

A.   1. better   2. condition
3. between   4. confirm
5. big   6. connect
7. bike   8. consider
9. bird   10. contain

B.   1. enough   2. even
3. equal   4. enter
5. graduate   6. great
7. grand

C.   1. need 2. learn
3. leave 4. never
5. negative 6. little
7. left

D.

Review TEST Day 041 ~ Day 045

• **Review TEST 1**

A.   1. bit   2. continue
3. black   4. control
5. block   6. conversation
7. blood   8. cook
9. blue   10. cool

B.   1. grow   2. ever
3. exact   4. event
5. group   6. green
7. sister

C.   1. lesson   2. less
3. next   4. noon
5. new   6. noise
7. letter

D.

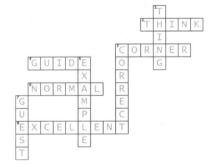

```
        G
        R
 B L O O D
 O        U
 C O N T R O L    B
 O        N        L
 T        D        A
 G R E E N       C O O K
 E                C
 W I S H        K
 I
 N
 P U L L
 E
```

• **Review TEST 2**

A.
1. board	2. copy
3. boat	4. corn
5. bone	6. corner
7. book	8. correct
9. born	10. cost

B.
1. except	2. exchange
3. excellent	4. guide
5. example	6. guess
7. excite	

C.
1. note	2. level
3. life	4. normal
5. lift	6. light
7. nothing	

D.

```
                    T
              T H I N K
              I
            C O R N E R
 G U I D E  O
        X   R
 N O R M A L R
 G      M   E
 U      P   C
 E X C E L L E N T
 S      E
 T
```

Review TEST Day 046 ~ Day 050

• **Review TEST 1**

A.
1. both	2. cotton
3. bottle	4. could
5. bottom	6. count
7. bought	8. bowl
9. course	10. country

B.
1. experience	2. expect
3. exercise	4. happen

---

5. throw	6. happy
7. half	

C.
1. notice	2. like
3. number	4. limited
5. list	6. link
7. now	

D.

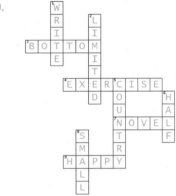

```
        W       L
        R       I
 B O T T O M    M
        I       I
        E       T
        E X E R C I S E
          D   O       H
              U       A
              N O V E L
          S   T       F
          M   R
 H A P P Y
          L
          L
```

• **Review TEST 2**

A.
1. box	2. cover
3. boy	4. cow
5. brain	6. creative
7. branch	8. crop
9. bread	10. cross

B.
1. have	2. express
3. face	4. hate
5. extra	6. hat
7. he	

C.
1. occur	2. observe
3. little	4. locate
5. object	6. ready
7. nurse	

D.

```
                F
                A
                C
 O       N U R S E      E
 B       E              X
 J       R    C O V E R A
 E    R  E              A
 C R E A T I V E
 T    A       V    E
      S       E    X
      O            P
 B R A N C H       R
                   E
                   S
                   S
```

MEMO

MEMO

MEMO